OODLES OF OPTIONS

THE SURVIVAL GUIDE TO LIFE OUTSIDE OF YOUR MOTHER'S KITCHEN

BY: RONALD A. MOSS II

Malcolm,

Good Luck as you

start this new chapter
in your life! Enjoy the book!

Remember you have
Oodles of Options!

THIS BOOK IS DEDICATED TO:
THE DREAMER IN ALL OF US

"WHAT IS YOUR PERSONAL CALLING? IT'S GOD'S BLESSING,
IT IS THE PATH GOD HAS CHOSEN FOR YOU HERE ON EARTH.
WHENEVER WE DO SOMETHING THAT FILLS US WITH
ENTHUSIASM WE ARE FOLLOWING OUR LEGEND.
HOWEVER, WE DO NOT ALL HAVE THE COURAGE TO CONFRONT
OUR OWN DREAM."
-PAOLO COELHO (*THE ALCHEMIST*)

BE COURAGEOUS AND FOLLOW YOUR DREAMS!

PREFACE

This cook book came about because I wanted to share what I had learned when I left home and I had to provide for myself. It was a time when I had to step out of my comfort zone. To me that was a place that many families create, that sense of home, unity, and love. A place that was centered around the foods of our many cultures, my mother's kitchen. I had to face the harsh reality that I now had to step up and sustain myself. I had my own place and no longer could I have the luxury of the "fine cuisine" in my university's cafeteria or food court. I now had to face life without a meal plan, which is real life in the real world. At this point I also made a decision that a diet of dollar menus and take-out Chinese food and $2 cheese steak platters would not be the best way to start a new phase of life living on my own. The basis of this book is a variety of dishes that have a pasta base, which for the most part is very inexpensive and can create a large amount of food. For the most frugal of diets Instant Ramen Noodles are a staple item. I am sure that at sometime in many people's lives they have had to consume a diet that consists of such. It is often referred to as the main element of a college student's diet, simply because of price, the amount of food it creates, and how easy it is to make. The variety of flavors now allow you to create all types of soup dishes, but coming from a history of high blood pressure, I had to watch my sodium intake. That being said I had to find a way to create dishes to break the monotony of just the plain noodles that I bought in bulk.

PREFACE CONT.

When I was learning how to cook the one thing that was instilled in me was that there is a base to cooking and it is all in the flavor and seasoning. The base that I most commonly learned was the use of GARLIC, ONIONS, AND PEPPERS. This is the heart and soul of most of the recipes you will find in this book. From that is where I began building these recipes. Some were inspired from popular dishes that I have had. Others came about when the ingredients were the only thing I had in my cupboards and/or fridge. It was these times that I made some things that I'd rather not mention but also ended up making some great dishes that all my friends loved. It was the joy that I found in creating these dishes, sometimes from hardly anything, that inspired me to write this book and share what I learned with you all. Even though I struggled to get out of this phase of my life like so many others, I can only look back and truly say that creativity truly comes from desperate times. These were the times where I was down to my last $5 dollars that I had to stretch for over a week. They were times when I was down to the last items in my cupboard and an empty fridge and even started contemplating eating those things that I buried deep in the pantry that I swore to never consume. These were the times where the recipes for this book were created but are not the only times when they can be useful to you. This will be your survival guide to creating cuisine on a very tight budget or a very lucrative one or like most of us, somewhere in between.

TABLE OF CONTENTS

1. HISTORY OF RAMEN NOODLES   H1-H2

2. KITCHEN SURVIVAL GUIDE   SG

3. CHICKEN RECIPES   C1-C10

4. BEEF RECIPES   B1-B10

5. PORK RECIPES   P1-P10

6. VEGGIE/MEATLESS RECIPIES   V1-V10

7. SEAFOOD RECIPES   S1-S10

8. CONTRIBUTED RECIPES   C11-C20

9. SPECIAL THANK YOU'S   ♥

10. ABOUT THE AUTHOR

TOC

history of ramen

Ramen is something that many may assume to be a Japanese dish, but it really originated in China. It started as a dish that was served in a broth mixed with vegetables and more than likely seafood as well. As it was adopted into a culture influenced by the western world a growing demand began to call for a meat base. Its origin is believed to be traced all the way back to the 17th century. As Chinese and Japanese cultures clashed and mixed Ramen was gradually introduced into the Japanese culture where it became staple dish to various regions of the island. The exact date as to its introduction is unknown, but what is known is that its popularity grew and this noodle became a common element in the diets of the Japanese people.

In the 1900s Ramen was a dish that was seen in many restaurants serving Chinese style dishes and it gained a reputation as a food that could be transported easily and served to the masses. It was served in the streets at portable food stalls to workers needing a quick meal. As it's popularity continued to grow, Ramen became common dish served at dine-in restaurants as well.

The traditional Ramen in its original form is not what we see today. Until the 1950s it more closely resembled what we consume in Chinese restaurants today known to us as Lo-Mein. There is a wide variety of Ramen served throughout Japan, but it was Instant Ramen that has had an impact on a global scale. It allowed millions of the culinary challenged to enjoy this dish as long as they were able to boil water or eventually use a microwave.

In 1957, a man by the name of Momofuku Ando (1910-2007) began experimenting with noodles and came to the conclusion that if he fried the noodles before they dried, they would instantly return to their state if placed in hot water. He revolutionized the way many people ate this popular dish and could quite possibly be one of the most widely used inventions in our modern culture. He experimented with this product when he was trying to find a way to feed the mass amount of the veterans after the war. This billon dollar industry sells a product that can be often found priced at $.08 for a single packet.

Many variations of Instant Ramen have been further developed and have spread far beyond Asia. In its variety of flavors, it has grown in popularity in various Latin American countries. Its interesting to see it in a grocery store in some of the places I have traveld in Africa, the Caribbean, Central and South America. In North America, Ramen is not really known by its original form, but rather as the instant noodles or soup cups that are stocked on nearly every grocer's shelves. From the 70's its growing popularity as an imported dish led to an implementation of manufacturer's in the US and by the mid 80s and it is now wildely known as a great food item for buyers that are on tight budgets. Also Ramen may always be considered the staple food of teens, college students and young professionals alike that are in need of quick, inexpensive meals.

work cited

http://en.wikipedia.org/wiki/Ramen

http://www.nissinfoods.com/company/about.php

http://www.konzak.com/ramen/ramhist.html

http://www.ramenlicious.com/encyclopedia/history-of-ramen.html

http://www.instantramen.or.jp/english/history/index.html

KITCHEN SURVIVAL GUIDE

IN THIS BOOK YOU WILL FIND A VARIETY OF DISHES THAT WILL EXCITE YOUR TASTE BUDS. TO REACH THAT POINT YOU MUST FIRST UNDERSTAND SOME OF THE KEYS TO MAKING FOOD TASTE GREAT CONSISTENTLY. THIS SECTION IS A GUIDE TO HELP YOU STOCK YOUR KITCHEN WITH ECONOMICAL AND PRACTICAL TOOLS, AND MOST IMPORTANTLY, BECOME FAMILIAR WITH THE CORE ELEMENTS OF SOME FLAVORFUL FOOD.

AS YOU READ ALONG INTO THE BOOK YOU WILL SEE THAT THERE IS SOMETHING THAT WILL BE A COMMON ELEMENT IN A MAJORITY OF THE RECIPES. IT IS WHAT I LIKE TO CALL THE

TRINITY OF FLAVOR!!!

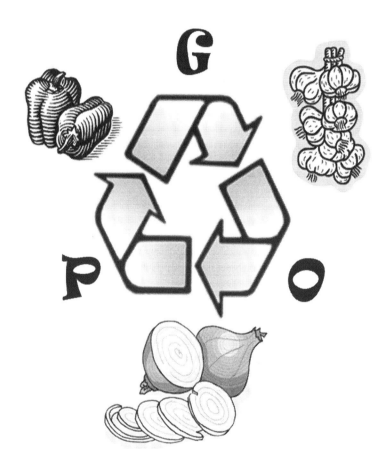

G.O.P. (GARLIC, ONIONS, & PEPPERS) ARE SOMETHING THAT I ALWAYS USE TO ADD FLAVOR TO ANYTHING FROM MEATS TO PASTA TO VEGETABLES. IT IS SOMETHING THAT IS INEXPENSIVE AND WILL MINIMIZE YOUR NEED TO PUT A LOT OF SALT IN YOUR FOODS. IT REALLY ENHANCES THE FLAVOR AND WILL MAKE YOUR DISHES QUITE TASTY. ONE THING I DO KNOW FOR SURE IS THAT PEOPLE DO NOT LIKE BLAND FOOD. ONCE YOU MASTER THE USE OF THE G.O.P. TRINITY, YOU CAN GUARANTEE THAT YOU WILL NOT HAVE THAT PROBLEM WHEN PEOPLE TRY YOUR COOKING.

STEPS TO A FLAVOR - FULL DISH

1. ALWAYS COOK WITH LOVE - THAT IS THE SECRET INGREDIENT IN THE FOOD YOU CRAVE THAT IS PREPARED BY SOMEONE CLOSE TO YOU.

2. KNOW THAT THE TRINITY IS YOUR FRIEND - THE FLAVOR THAT IT BRINGS TO YOUR DISH AND HOW THEY HARMONIZE WILL MAKE ALL YOUR FOOD TASTE GREAT!

3. UNDERSTAND THAT FLAVOR DOES NOT ONLY COME FROM SALT.

4. DO NOT BE AFRAID TO HAVE FUN IN THE KITCHEN.

5. BE CREATIVE AND TRY DIFFERENT THINGS.

SEASONINGS

THIS DOES NOT MEAN SALT : USE VARIETIES OF SPICES AND SEASONINGS AND YOUR FOOD WILL ALWAYS LEAVE YOU SATISFIED.

USE FRESH HERBS: IF YOU LIKE TO GROW THINGS TRY GROWING YOUR OWN HERBS. THE FRESHNESS OF YOUR HERBS WILL TAKE THE FLAVORS OF YOUR DISHES TO A WHOLE NEW LEVEL.

SEASONING MEAT: WHEN COOKING DIFFERENT TYPES OF MEAT, IT IS HELPFUL USE SEASONING THAT IS SPECIFIC TO THAT PARTICULAR MEAT. FOR EXAMPLE, STEAK SEASONING, CHICKEN AND POULTRY RUB, AND CAJUN BLEND PORK SEASONING ARE CONVINIENT, BUT A SEASON ALL(ADOBO, SEASON SALT) WILL WORK JUST FINE.

MARINATING: THE KEY TO MOST MEAT DISHES IS IN THE MARINADE. GREAT ONES TO USE ARE WINE, BEER, OR ANY OTHER ALCOHOLIC BEVERAGE. IT HELPS TO TENDERIZE THE MEAT. YOU CAN ALSO USE MARINADE BLENDS TO ADD A SPECIFIC FLAVOR TO THE MEAT DISHES: FOR EXAMPLE TERIYAKI, GARLIC& HERB, ETC. WHEN YOU MIX THESE WITH THE DRY SEASONINGS AND G.O.P. YOU WILL HAVE DISHES WITH UNSTOPPABLE FLAVOR

VEGGIES

GO FRESH: VEGETABLES THAT ARE STRAIGHT FROM THE GROCER'S PRODUCE SECTION OR THE FARMER'S MARKET ARE GREAT FOR PREPAPRING FRESH MEALS. NOW, IF YOU DON'T COOK OFTEN, GET FROZEN AND USE ONLY WHAT YOU NEED; LEAVE THE REST FROZEN. DON'T FREEZE, THAW, THEN FREEZE AGAIN

MEATS

GO LEAN: GET TO KNOW THE BUTCHER AT YOUR LOCAL GROCERY STORE FOR RECCOMENDATIONSON THE RIGHT CUTS TO USE FOR VARIOUS DISHES. ALWAYS CHECK THE DATES.

COOKWARE

THIS IS THE PLACE WHERE ALL THE MAGIC HAPPENS. YOUR COOKWEAR IS THE PLACE
WHERE ALL THE FLAVORS, ENERGY, AND LOVE COME TOGETHER.

FOR SAUTEEING : THESE RECIPIES CALL FOR SMALL AMOUNTS OF COOKING, SO
A NON STICK OR STAINLESS STEEL FRYING PAN

FOR BOILING : USE VARYING SIZES OF POTS (ALUMINUM/STAINLESS STEEL POTS)

FOR BAKING: CORNINGWEAR CASSEROLE DISHES WORK AND ARE EASY TO CLEAN.
WHEN SERVING LARGER GROUPS OF PEOPLE, THE DISPOSABLE
ALUMINUM PANS WORK WELL AND THE CAN BE RECYLCLED OR REUSED.

UTENSILS

THESE ARE THE TOOLS THAT BUILD ALL THE DISHES THAT YOU CREATE. THEIR USE PLAYS
A MAJOR ROLE IN, COOKING AND SERVING, ALL OF WHICH ARE THE STEPS TO
BRINGING THESE DISHES TO THE PLACE THEY LONG TO GO...
YOUR MOUTH!!

PREP: A GOOD KNIFE SET IS REALLY HELPFUL FOR CUTTING DIFFERENT
TYPES OF MEATS AND VEGGIES. ALSO A SOLID CUTTING BOARD WILL HELP
KEEP YOUR COUNTERTOPS IN GOOD SHAPE.

COOKING: WOODEN SPOONS WILL WORK WELL FOR SAUTEEING AND
ALSO STIRRING THE NOODLES AS THEY BOIL.

SERVING: PLASTIC SPATULAS AND SPOONS PROVIDE A LARGE SURFACE AREA
THAT IS GOOD FOR SCOOPING AND SERVING THE GREAT DISHES THAT
YOU WILL CREATE AS YOU EXPLORE THIS BOOK.

SG

Oodles of Options

Chicken Recipes

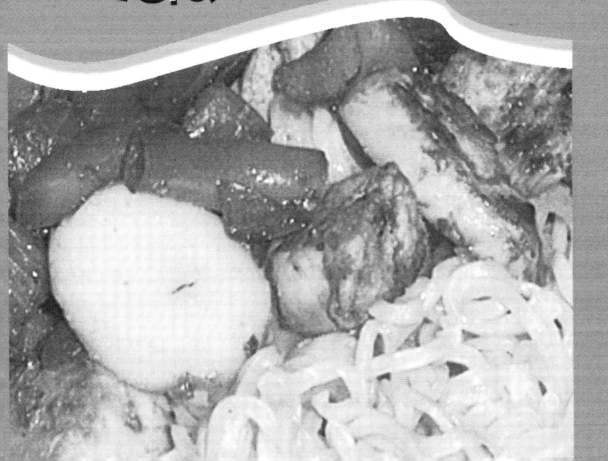

NOTES

CHICKEN CUTLETS WITH RED BEANS

INGREDIENTS:
- 1 CLOVE -DICED GARLIC ⎫ G.O.P.
- ½ CUP - DICED ONIONS   ⎬
- ½ CUP - DICED PEPPERS   ⎭
- 4 SLICED - BONELESS CHICKEN CUTLETS
- 1 CAN - RED BEANS, DRAINED
- SEASON ALL (TO TASTE)
- 3 CUPS - WATER
- 2 PACKAGES - RAMEN NOODLES
- 1 TABLESPOON - EXTRA VIRGIN OLIVE OIL

DIRECTIONS:
1. IN A LARGE FRYING PAN COOK THE G.O.P.. WITH OLIVE OIL UNTIL BROWNED

2. SPRINKLE CHICKEN CUTLETS WITH SEASON ALL AND ADD TO THE PAN. BROWN ON ALL SIDES.

3. ONCE THE CHICKEN IS COOKED ADD THE CAN OF BEANS AND COOK ON HIGH HEAT FOR 5-10 MINUTES. THEN LET IT SIMMER.

4. IN ANOTHER PAN ADD 3 CUPS OF WATER AND BRING TO BOIL. BREAK UP THE PACKAGES OF RAMEN AND ADD TO THE BOILING WATER

5. COOK THE NOODLES UNTIL TENDER BUT STILL FIRM, STIRRING ONCE OR TWICE TO BREAK APART. DRAIN WELL, AND PLATE THEN DRIZZLE WITH OLIVE OIL.

6. TOP THE NOODLES WITH THE CHICKEN AND BEANS.

NOTES

PESTO CHICKEN NOODLES

INGREDIENTS:

- 1 TABLESPOON - EXTRA VIRGIN OLIVE OIL
- 1 CLOVE - DICED GARLIC
- ½ CUP - DICED ONIONS   } G.O.P.
- ½ CUP - DICED PEPPERS
- 2 PACKAGES OF RAMEN NOODLES
- 2 SLICED - BONELESS CHICKEN BREASTS, 1/4" THIN STRIPS
- SEASON ALL - TO TASTE
- 3 CUPS - WATER
- 3 - 4 TABLESPOONS BASIL PESTO
- SEASON ALL - TO TASTE
- GRATED PARMESAN AND/OR ROMANO CHEESE - TO TASTE

DIRECTIONS:

1. IN A LARGE FRYING PAN COOK THE G.O.P. WITH THE OLIVE OIL SPRINKLE CHICKEN SLICES WITH SEASON ALL AND BROWN ON ALL SIDES. ONCE BROWNED REDUCE HEAT TO SIMMER UNTIL NOODLES ARE FINISHED.

2. IN ANOTHER PAN ADD 3 CUPS OF WATER AND BRING TO BOIL BREAK UP THE PACKAGES OF RAMEN AND ADD TO THE BOILING WATER

3. COOK THE NOODLES UNTIL TENDER BUT STILL FIRM, STIRRING ONCE OR TWICE TO BREAK APART. DRAIN WELL AND ADD TO PAN WITH THE CHICKEN

4. STIR IN THE PESTO AND BRING TO A MEDIUM HEAT FOR 2-3 MINUTES.

5. ONCE HEATED AND COATED WELL SERVE ON A PLATE AND TOP WITH THE GRATED CHEESE.

NOTES

CHICKEN FAJITA NOODLES

INGREDIENTS:
* 1 CLOVE - DICED GARLIC
* ½ CUP - DICED ONIONS   } G.O.P.
* ½ CUP - DICED PEPPERS
  (GREEN, RED, AND/OR YELLOW)
* 4 SLICED - BONELESS CHICKEN CUTLETS
* SEASON ALL - TO TASTE
* 2 PACKAGES OF RAMEN NOODLES
* 3 CUPS - WATER
* SALSA
* SHREDDED CHEESE (MOZZARELLA, CHEDDAR, MONTERREY JACK)

DIRECTIONS:

1. IN A LARGE FRYING PAN COOK THE G.O.P. WITH THE OLIVE OIL SPRINKLE
   CHICKEN SLICES WITH SEASON ALL AND BROWN ON ALL SIDES. ONCE
   BROWNED REDUCE HEAT AND KEEP WARM UNTIL NOODLES ARE FINISHED.

2. IN ANOTHER POT ADD 3 CUPS OF WATER AND BRING TO BOIL. BREAK
   UP THE PACKAGES OF RAMEN AND ADD TO THE BOILING WATER

3. COOK THE NOODLES UNTIL TENDER BUT STILL FIRM, STIRRING ONCE
   OR TWICE TO BREAK APART. DRAIN WELL

4. SET THE NOODLES INTO THE PAN WITH THE CHICKEN AND G.O.P. MIXTURE,
   AND STIR IN THE SALSA

5. PLACED THE COMBINED ELEMENTS ONTO A PLATE AND SPRINKLE
   THE CHEESE OVER THE DISH.

C3

NOTES

CHICKEN ALFREDO

INGREDIENTS:

- 2 SLICED BONELESS CHICKEN BREASTS
- SEASON ALL , BASIL, OREGANO, ITALIAN SEASONING – TO TASTE
- 1 TABLESPOON – EXTRA VIRGIN OLIVE OIL
- 1 CLOVE – DICED GARLIC
- 2 PACKAGES – RAMEN NOODLES
- 2 CUPS – WATER
- 1 16 OZ JAR – ALFREDO SAUCE
- 1 –1/2 CUP – ASSORTED CHEESES, GRATED OR SHREDDED
  (EX. ROMANO, PARMESAN, ASIAGO, AND/OR PROVOLONE)

DIRECTIONS:

1. START BY SEASONING THE CHICKEN WITH YOUR CHOICE OF SPICES OR YOUR FAVORITE SEASON ALL

2. IN A LARGE SAUCE PAN COOK THE GARLIC WITH THE OLIVE OIL AND CHICKEN SLICES AND BROWN ON ALL SIDES. ONCE BROWNED KEEP WARM UNTIL NOODLES ARE FINISHED.

3. IN ANOTHER PAN ADD 3 CUPS OF WATER AND BRING TO BOIL. BREAK UP THE PACKAGES OF RAMEN AND ADD TO THE BOILING WATER

4. WHILE THE NOODLES ARE BOILING ADD THE SAUCE AND CHEESE TO THE PAN WITH THE CHICKEN AND COOK AT A LOW HEAT. STIR UNTIL IT IS THICKENED AND CREAMY IF NEEDED.

5. COOK THE NOODLES UNTIL TENDER BUT STILL FIRM, STIRRING ONCE OR TWICE TO BREAK APART. DRAIN WELL AND ADD TO PAN WITH THE CHICKEN AND CHEESE SAUCE

6. THEN MIX EVERYTHING ALL TOGETHER AT A MEDIUM HEAT.

7. ONCE HEATED AND MIXED WELL SERVE ON A PLATE.

C4

NOTES

TERIYAKI CHICKEN

INGREDIENTS:

- 2 SLICED - BONELESS CHICKEN BREASTS
- 2 TABLESPOONS - TERIYAKI MARINADE
- SEASON ALL , BASIL, OREGANO- TO TASTE
- 1 CLOVE - DICED GARLIC
- ½ CUP - DICED ONIONS   } G.O.P.
- ½ CUP - DICED PEPPERS
- 1 CUP MIXED VEGETABLES
- 2 PACKAGES - RAMEN NOODLES
- 2 CUPS - WATER
- 1 TABLESPOON - EXTRA VIRGIN OLIVE OIL

DIRECTIONS:

1. START BY SEASONING THE CHICKEN WITH YOUR FAVORITE SEASON ALL
   WITH SOME BASIL AND OREGANO AND TERIYAKI MARINADE. YOU CAN
   MARINATE 24 HOURS (MIN. 1 HOUR) PRIOR TO COOKING. NOTE THE LONGER
   YOU MARINATE THE MEAT IT WILL ABSORB MORE OF THE FLAVOR.

2. IN A LARGE FRYING PAN COOK THE G.O.P. WITH THE OLIVE OIL MIXED
   VEGETABLES AND CHICKEN SLICES (ADD MORE SAUCE IF NEEDED) AND
   BROWN ON ALL SIDES.

3. ONCE BROWNED PLACE ON SIMMER UNTIL NOODLES ARE FINISHED.

4. IN ANOTHER PAN ADD 3 CUPS OF WATER AND BRING TO BOIL. BREAK
   UP THE PACKAGES OF RAMEN AND ADD TO THE BOILING WATER

5. COOK THE NOODLES UNTIL TENDER BUT STILL FIRM, STIRRING ONCE
   OR TWICE TO BREAK APART. DRAIN WELL AND ADD TO PAN WITH
   THE CHICKEN AND TERIYAKI SAUCE MIXTURE.

6. MIX WELL AT A MEDIUM HEAT AND THEN SERVE ON A PLATE.

NOTES

MEDITERRANEAN CHICKEN

INGREDIENTS:

- 4 SLICED – BONELESS CHICKEN CUTLETS, 1/4" THIN STRIPS
- SEASON ALL – TO TASTE
- BASIL & OREGANO – TO TASTE
- 1 TABLESPOON – BALSAMIC VINAIGRETTE
- 2 TABLESPOONS – EXTRA VIRGIN OLIVE OIL
- 1 CLOVE – DICED GARLIC } G.O.P.
- ½ CUP – DICED ONIONS
- ½ CUP – DICED PEPPERS
- 2 PACKAGES – RAMEN NOODLES
- 3 CUPS – WATER
- ½ CUP – FETA CHEESE
- GARLIC POWDER – TO TASTE

DIRECTIONS:

1. START BY SEASONING THE CHICKEN WITH YOUR FAVORITE SEASON ALL AND MARINATE WITH THE BALSAMIC VINAIGRETTE. YOU CAN MARINATE UP TO 24 HOURS (MIN. 1 HOUR) PRIOR TO COOKING. NOTE THE LONGER YOU MARINATE THE MEAT IT WILL ABSORB MORE OF THE FLAVOR.

2. IN A LARGE FRYING PAN COOK THE G.O.P. WITH THE OLIVE OIL, AND CHICKEN SLICES. ADD IN THE POTATOES BROWN ON ALL SIDES. WHILE COOKING SPRINKLE BASIL, AND OREGANO ATOP THE MIXTURE. ONCE BROWNED PLACE ON SIMMER UNTIL NOODLES ARE FINISHED.

3. IN THE SAUCE PAN PAN ADD 3 CUPS OF WATER AND BRING TO BOIL. BREAK UP THE PACKAGES OF RAMEN AND ADD TO THE BOILING WATER

4. COOK THE NOODLES UNTIL TENDER BUT STILL FIRM, STIRRING ONCE OR TWICE TO BREAK APART. DRAIN WELL

5. ONCE THE NOODLES ARE FINISHED SET THEM ONTO THE PLATE AND TOP WITH SOME OREGANO AND GARLIC POWDER AND THE CHICKEN AND BALSAMIC VINAIGRETTE MIXTURE.

6. TOP THE DISH WITH FETA CHEESE AND GARNISH WITH BASIL.

NOTES

LEMON PEPPER CHICKEN

INGREDIENTS:

- 2 BONELESS CHICKEN BREASTS CUT INTO 1/2" PIECES
- LEMON PEPPER SEASONING - TO TASTE
- 1 TABLESPOON - EXTRA VIRGIN OLIVE OIL
- 1 CLOVE - DICED GARLIC
- ½ CUP - DICED ONIONS   } G.O.P.
- ½ CUP - DICED PEPPERS
- 1 CUP - MIXED VEGETABLES
- 2 PACKAGES - RAMEN NOODLES
- 3 CUPS - WATER
- 3 TABLESPOONS -LEMON PEPPER MARINADE

DIRECTIONS:

1. START BY SEASONING THE CHICKEN WITH THE LEMON PEPPER SEASONING

2. IN A LARGE FRYING PAN COOK THE G.O.P. WITH THE OLIVE OIL, CHICKEN, AND MIXED VEGETABLES, COOK UNTIL BROWN ON ALL SIDES. ONCE BROWNED PLACE ON SIMMER UNTIL NOODLES ARE FINISHED.

3. IN A SAUCE PAN PAN ADD 3 CUPS OF WATER AND BRING TO BOIL. BREAK UP THE PACKAGES OF RAMEN AND ADD TO THE BOILING WATER

4. COOK THE NOODLES UNTIL TENDER BUT STILL FIRM, STIRRING ONCE OR TWICE TO BREAK APART. DRAIN WELL. ONCE NOODLES ARE FINISHED DRAINING SET THEM INTO THE PAN WITH THE CHICKEN AND MIX IN LEMON PEPPER MARINADE AND THOROUGHLY MIX TOGETHER OVER A MEDIUM HEAT.

5. ONCE HEATED AND MIXED SERVE ON A PLATE.

NOTES

CHICKEN WITH GARLIC SAUCE

INGREDIENTS:

- 4 BONELESS CHICKEN CUTLETS, CHOPPED IN 1/2" PIECES
- SEASON ALL AND GARLIC POWDER - TO TASTE
- 1 TABLESPOON - EXTRA VIRGIN OLIVE OIL
- 1 CLOVE - DICED GARLIC
- ½ CUP - DICED ONIONS   } G.O.P.
- ½ CUP - DICED PEPPERS
- 4 TABLESPOONS - GARLIC AND HERB MARINADE
- 1 CUP - MIXED VEGETABLES
- 2 PACKAGES - RAMEN NOODLES
- 3 CUPS - WATER

DIRECTIONS:

1. START BY SEASONING THE CHICKEN WITH THE GARLIC POWDER AND SEASON ALL ON ALL SIDES.

2. IN A LARGE FRYING PAN COOK THE G.O.P. WITH THE OLIVE OIL AND CHICKEN UNTIL BROWNED. ADD GARLIC AND HERB MARINADE, AND MIXED VEGETABLES TO CREATE SAUCE, PLACE ON SIMMER UNTIL NOODLES ARE FINISHED.

3. IN A SAUCE PAN ADD 3 CUPS OF WATER AND BRING TO BOIL. BREAK UP THE PACKAGES OF RAMEN AND ADD TO THE BOILING WATER

4. COOK THE NOODLES UNTIL TENDER BUT STILL FIRM, STIRRING ONCE OR TWICE TO BREAK APART. DRAIN WELL. ONCE NOODLES ARE FINISHED DRAINING, SET THEM INTO THE PAN WITH THE CHICKEN AND GARLIC SAUCE AND MIX ALL THE INGREDIENTS TOGETHER OVER A MEDIUM HEAT UNTIL THE NOODLES ARE COATED. ADD MORE MARINADE IF NEEDED.

5. ONCE HEATED AND MIXED, SERVE ON A PLATE.

NOTES

NOODLES CON POLLO

INGREDIENTS:

- 1 CLOVE - DICED GARLIC
- ½ CUP - DICED ONIONS   } G.O.P.
- ½ CUP - DICED PEPPERS
- SEASON ALL - TO TASTE
- 1 TABLESPOON - EXTRA VIRGIN OLIVE OIL
- 1 FRESH TOMATO - CUT AND CUBED
- ½ CAN (8OZ) - TOMATO SAUCE
- 6 OUNCES - BEER OR COOKING WINE
- 4 BONELESS CHICKEN CUTLETS, SLICED INTO CHOPPED 1/4" PIECES
- 1/2 TEA SPOON - GROUND CUMIN
- 2 PACKAGES - RAMEN NOODLES
- 2 CUPS - CHICKEN BROTH
- ¼ CUP - OLIVES
- 1 CAN - PEAS (DRAINED)

DIRECTIONS:

1. IN A LARGE SAUCE PAN COOK G.O.P. WITH OLIVE OIL UNTIL BROWNED.

2. ADD THE TOMATOES, THE TOMATO SAUCE, AND THE WINE OR BEER

3. ADD SLICES OF CHICKEN CUTLETS TO THE PAN ALONG WITH THE CUMIN AND SEASON ALL.

4. ADD 2 CUPS OF CHICKEN BROTH TO ANOTHER POT AND BRING TO BOIL BREAK UP THE PACKAGES OF RAMEN AND ADD TO THE BROTH.

5. ONCE THE CHICKEN IS ALMOST COOKED LOWER THE HEAT AND LET IT SIMMER.

6. COOK THE NOODLES UNTIL TENDER BUT STILL FIRM, STIRRING ONCE OR TWICE TO BREAK APART.

7. ONCE THEY ARE DONE ADD THE NOODLES AND BROTH TO THE POT WITH THE CHICKEN AND SAUCE AND OLIVES, AND PEAS.

8. CONTINUE TO STIR ON A LOW HEAT AND MIX UNTIL IT THICKENS. AND THEN SERVE.

NOTES

CURRY CHICKEN NOODLES

INGREDIENTS:

- 3 TABLE SPOONS OF CURRY POWDER
- ½ CUP - OLIVE OIL
- 1 CLOVE - DICED GARLIC
- ½ CUP - DICED ONIONS   } G.O.P.
- ½ CUP - DICED PEPPERS
- 1-2 POTATOES - CUBED AND BOILED
- 2 PACKAGES - RAMEN NOODLES
- 3 CUPS - WATER
- 4 BONELESS CHICKEN CUTLETS, SLICED IN 1/4" STRIPS
- SEASON ALL -TO TASTE
- 1 CUP - CRUSHED FRESH TOMATOES

DIRECTIONS:

1. IN A BOWL MIX UP THE CURRY POWER AND 1/2 A CUP OF WATER AND MIX WELL UNTIL IT TURNS INTO A PASTE.

2. IN A LARGE FRYING PAN SAUTÉ THE CURRY POWDER, AND OIL VERY WELL FOR AT LEAST 10 MINUTES. ADD WATER AS NEEDED TO KEEP IT FROM BURNING.

3. ADD THE G.O.P TO THE PAN AND COOK UNTIL BROWNED.

4. IN A SAUCE PAN ADD 3 CUPS OF WATER TO ANOTHER POT AND BRING TO BOIL. ADD THE CUBED POTATOES AND BREAK UP NOODLES. ADD THE POTATOES FIRST AND COOK UNTIL SOFTENED AND THEN ADD THE NOODLES.

5. COOK THE NOODLES UNTIL TENDER BUT STILL FIRM, STIRRING ONCE OR TWICE TO BREAK APART. DRAIN WELL.

6. SPRINKLE SEASON ALL ON THE SLICES OF CHICKEN CUTLETS AND ADD TO THE PAN OF G.O.P AND CURRY ALONG WITH THE CRUSHED TOMATOES.

7. ONCE THE CHICKEN IS COOKED ADD THE NOODLES TO THE SAUCE MIXTURE. AND STIR TOGETHER, THEN LET IT SIMMER. SERVE IN BOWLS.

Oodles of Options

Beef Recipes

NOTES

TACO NOODLES

INGREDIENTS:

- 2 CLOVES DICED GARLIC ⎫
- 1 CUP DICED ONIONS   ⎬ G.O.P.
- ½ CUP DICED PEPPERS   ⎭
- 2 PACKAGES - RAMEN NOODLES
- 3 CUPS - WATER
- ½ POUND - GROUND BEEF
- 1 CUP TOMATOES -DICED
- 1 CUP LETTUCE - SHREDDED
- ¼ CUP - SHREDDED CHEDDAR CHEESE
- 1 TABLE SPOON - SOUR CREAM
- SEASON ALL - TO TASTE
- 1 TABLESPOON -EXTRA VIRGIN OLIVE OIL

DIRECTIONS:

1. IN A LARGE FRYING PAN COOK THE G.O.P. (1 CLOVE OF DICED GARLIC AND 1/2 CUP OF ONIONS AND THE PEPPERS) WITH OLIVE OIL UNTIL BROWNED

2. ADD THE GROUND BEEF TO THE PAN ALONG WITH SEASON ALL AND COOK UNTIL BROWNED AND DRAIN THE GREASE.

3. IN A SMALL SALAD BOWL, TOSS THE REST OF THE ONIONS, GARLIC, TOMATOES, GARLIC, AND OLIVE OIL AND MIX IT ALL UP IN A BOWL TO CREATE A SALSA

4. IN ANOTHER POT ADD 3 CUPS OF WATER AND BRING TO BOIL AND BREAK UP THE PACKAGES OF NOODLES AND ADD TO BOILING WATER.

5. COOK THE NOODLES UNTIL TENDER BUT STILL FIRM, STIRRING ONCE OR TWICE TO BREAK APART. DRAIN WELL, AND PLATE THEN DRIZZLE WITH OLIVE OIL.

6. AFTER YOU SET A BED OF NOODLES ON A PLATE, TOP WITH THE LETTUCE AND THE GROUND BEEF MIXTURE.

7. TOP WITH THE SALSA AND SPRINKLE THE CHEDDAR CHEESE AND ADD SOME SOUR CREAM.

NOTES

SPAGHETTI NOODLES

INGREDIENTS:

- 1 CLOVE - DICED GARLIC ⎫
- ½ CUP - DICED ONIONS   ⎬ G.O.P.
- ½ CUP - DICED PEPPERS   ⎭
- 2 PACKAGES - RAMEN NOODLES
- 3 CUPS - WATER
- 16 OZ. - GROUND BEEF
- 3 CUPS OF YOUR FAVORITE SPAGHETTI SAUCE - ABOUT 24 OZ.
- SEASON ALL - TO TASTE
- 1 TABLESPOON - EXTRA VIRGIN OLIVE OIL

DIRECTIONS:

1. IN A LARGE FRYING PAN COOK THE G.O.P. WITH OLIVE OIL UNTIL BROWNED

2. ADD THE GROUND BEEF TO THE PAN ALONG WITH SEASON ALL AND COOK UNTIL BROWNED AND THEN DRAIN THE GREASE.

3. IN ANOTHER POT ADD 3 CUPS OF WATER AND BRING TO BOIL. BREAK UP THE PACKAGES OF RAMEN AND ADD TO THE BOILING WATER

4. ONCE THE GROUND BEEF IS COOKED ADD THE 3 CUPS OF SPAGHETTI SAUCE AND KEEP IN ON HIGH HEAT FOR ABOUT 5 MINUTES OR UNTIL BUBBLING. THEN LET IT SIMMER.

5. COOK THE NOODLES UNTIL TENDER BUT STILL FIRM, STIRRING ONCE OR TWICE TO BREAK APART. DRAIN WELL.

6. SET A BED OF NOODLES ON A PLATE THEN DRIZZLE WITH OLIVE OIL AND TOP WITH THE MEAT SAUCE.

NOTES

CHILI N' NOODLES

INGREDIENTS:

- ❈ 1 CLOVE - DICED GARLIC
- ❈ ½ CUP - DICED ONIONS   } G.O.P.
- ❈ ½ CUP - DICED PEPPERS
- ❈ 2 PACKAGES - RAMEN NOODLES
- ❈ 3 CUPS - OF WATER
- ❈ 1/2 LB. - GROUND BEEF
- ❈ 1 15 OZ. CAN - RED BEANS- DRAINED
- ❈ SEASON ALL-TO TASTE
- ❈ 1 TABLESPOON - EXTRA VIRGIN OLIVE OIL
- ❈ 1/2 10 OZ. CAN - TOMATO SAUCE
- ❈ 1 PACKET - CHILI POWDER

DIRECTIONS:

1. IN A LARGE FRYING PAN COOK THE G.O.P. WITH OLIVE OIL UNTIL BROWNED

2. ADD THE GROUND BEEF TO THE PAN ALONG WITH SEASON ALL AND COOK UNTIL BROWNED AND THEN DRAIN THE GREASE.

3. IN ANOTHER POT ADD 3 CUPS OF WATER AND BRING TO BOIL. BREAK UP THE PACKAGES OF RAMEN AND ADD TO THE BOILING WATER

4. ONCE THE GROUND BEEF IS COOKED ADD THE CAN OF BEANS TOMATO SAUCE, AND CHILI POWDER AND KEEP IN ON HIGH HEAT FOR 5- 10 MINUTES. THEN LET IT SIMMER.

5. COOK THE NOODLES UNTIL TENDER BUT STILL FIRM, STIRRING ONCE OR TWICE TO BREAK APART. DRAIN WELL.

6. SET A BED OF NOODLES ON A PLATE THEN DRIZZLE WITH OLIVE OIL AND TOP WITH THE CHILI.

B3

NOTES

CHEESE STEAK NOODLES

INGREDIENTS:

* 1 CLOVE - DICED GARLIC
* ½ CUP - DICED ONIONS   } G.O.P.
* ½ CUP - DICED PEPPERS
* 2 PACKAGES - RAMEN NOODLES
* 3 CUPS - WATER
* 8 OZ.- FROZEN STEAK STRIPS OR THICK CUTS OF ROAST BEEF
* 1 TABLESPOON - EXTRA VIRGIN OLIVE OIL
* 1 TEASPOON - STEAK SEASONING AND WORCHESTER SAUCE
* CHEESE: AMERICAN, PROVOLONE(4 SLICES), OR MELTED CHEDDAR (1 CUP)

* OPTIONAL: LONG HOAGIE ROLL WITH LETTUCE AND TOMATOES*

DIRECTIONS:

1. IN A LARGE FRYING PAN COOK THE G.O.P. WITH OLIVE OIL
   UNTIL BROWNED

2. ADD SLICES OF STEAK TO THE PAN WITH THE G.O.P. ALONG WITH
   STEAK SEASONING AND WORCHESTER SAUCE.

3. IN ANOTHER POT ADD 3 CUPS OF WATER AND BRING TO BOIL. BREAK
   UP THE PACKAGES OF RAMEN AND ADD TO THE BOILING WATER

4. COOK THE NOODLES UNTIL TENDER BUT STILL FIRM, STIRRING ONCE
   OR TWICE TO BREAK APART. DRAIN WELL, AND SET THEM BACK IN THE
   POT AND MIX IN THE MELTED CHEDDAR OR SLICES OF CHEESE UNTIL THE
   NOODLES ARE COATED.

5. SET A BED OF CHEESY NOODLES ON A PLATE THEN TOP WITH THE STEAK.

* TO CREATE IN THE ACTUAL CHEESE STEAK HOAGIE FORM, PLACE MEAT AND
   NOODLES INTO THE ROLL AND ADD LETTUCE AND TOMATOES AND
   CONDIMENTS OF CHOICE.

B4

NOTES

BEEF AND BROCCOLI

INGREDIENTS:

- 1 CLOVE - DICED GARLIC
- ½ CUP - DICED ONIONS ⎫ G.O.P.
- ½ CUP - DICED PEPPERS ⎭
- 2 PACKAGES - RAMEN NOODLES
- 3 CUPS - WATER
- ½ LB. STEAK SLICED, 1/4" STRIPS
- 1 TABLESPOON - EXTRA VIRGIN OLIVE OIL
- 1 TEASPOON - STEAK SEASONING/WORCHESTER SAUCE
- ½ BAG –FROZEN BROCCOLI
- 1 TEASPOON - SOY SAUCE

DIRECTIONS:

1. IN A LARGE FRYING PAN COOK THE G.O.P. WITH OLIVE OIL
   UNTIL BROWNED

2. ADD SLICES OF STEAK TO THE PAN WITH THE G.O.P. ALONG
   WITH STEAK SEASONING AND/OR WORCHESTER SAUCE AND SOY SAUCE.

3. IN ANOTHER POT ADD 3 CUPS OF WATER AND BRING TO BOIL. BREAK
   UP THE PACKAGES OF RAMEN AND ADD TO THE BOILING WATER

4. ONCE THE STEAK IS COOKED ADD THE BROCCOLI AND COOK UNTIL
   HOT AND STILL CRISP

5. COOK THE NOODLES UNTIL TENDER BUT STILL FIRM, STIRRING ONCE
   OR TWICE TO BREAK APART. DRAIN WELL.

6. SET A BED OF NOODLES ON A PLATE THEN DRIZZLE WITH OLIVE OIL.
    OR SOY SAUCE, THEN TOP WITH BEEF AND BROCCOLI.

NOTES

PEPPER STEAK

INGREDIENTS:

- ❊ 1 CLOVE - DICED GARLIC
- ❊ ½ CUP - DICED ONIONS   } G.O.P.
- ❊ ½ CUP - DICED PEPPERS
  (TRY A VARIETY FOR COLOR: YELLOW RED AND GREEN)
- ❊ 2 PACKAGES - RAMEN NOODLES
- ❊ 3 CUPS - WATER
- ❊ ½ LB. - STEAK STRIPS
- ❊ 1 TABLESPOON - EXTRA VIRGIN OLIVE OIL
- ❊ 1 TABLESPOON - CRUSHED RED PEPPER
- ❊ 1 TABLESPOON - CUMIN
- ❊ 1 TABLESPOON - A1 STEAK SAUCE

DIRECTIONS:

1. IN A LARGE FRYING PAN COOK THE G.O.P. WITH OLIVE OIL UNTIL BROWNED

2. ADD SLICES OF STEAK TO THE PAN WITH THE G.O.P. ALONG WITH CRUSHED PEPPER AND CUMIN AND STEAK SAUCE AND COOK UNTIL COOKED THRU WELL.

3. IN ANOTHER POT ADD 3 CUPS OF WATER AND BRING TO BOIL. BREAK UP THE PACKAGES OF RAMEN AND ADD TO THE BOILING WATER

4. COOK THE NOODLES UNTIL TENDER BUT STILL FIRM, STIRRING ONCE OR TWICE TO BREAK APART. DRAIN WELL

5. SET A BED OF NOODLES ON A PLATE AND DRIZZLE WITH OLIVE OIL THEN TOP STEAK AND PEPPERS MIXTURE.

B6

NOTES

COUNTRY FRIED STEAK

INGREDIENTS:

- 1 CLOVE - DICED GARLIC
- ½ CUP - DICED ONIONS   } G.O.P.
- ½ CUP - DICED PEPPERS
- 2 PACKAGES - RAMEN NOODLES
- 3 CUPS - WATER
- ½ LB. - SIRLOIN STEAK
- 1 TABLESPOON - EXTRA VIRGIN OLIVE OIL
- 2 TABLESPOONS - STEAK MARINADE
- 1 TEASPOON - STEAK SEASONING
- ITALIAN BREAD CRUMBS
- 1-2 EGGS
- 8 OZ. - COUNTRY FRIED STEAK GRAVY

DIRECTIONS:

1. PREP: MARINATE THE STEAKS BY THOROUGHLY COATING THE STEAKS WITH THE STEAK MARINADE.
   WHISK THE EGGS IN A BOWL AND ADD SOME STEAK SEASONING AS YOU WHISK.

2. DIP THE STEAK(S) IN THE EGG ON ALL SIDES UNTIL COVERED

3. COAT THE STEAK(S) WITH THE BREAD CRUMBS.

4. IN A LARGE FRYING PAN COOK THE G.O.P. WITH OLIVE OIL UNTIL BROWNED THEN SET TO THE SIDE.

5. PREHEAT ANOTHER PAN WITH OIL FOR FRYING.

6. IN ANOTHER POT ADD 3 CUPS OF WATER AND BRING TO BOIL. BREAK UP THE PACKAGES OF RAMEN AND ADD TO THE BOILING WATER

7. ONCE THE STEAK IS BREADED, PLACE THEM THE OIL AND FRY UNTIL BROWNED AND FULLY COOKED INSIDE. THEN LET THEM COOL AND THEN SLICE INTO STRIPS.

8. HEAT UP GRAVY

9. COOK THE NOODLES UNTIL TENDER BUT STILL FIRM, STIRRING ONCE OR TWICE TO BREAK APART. DRAIN WELL.

10. SET A BED OF NOODLES ON THE PLATE AND THEN ADD THE STRIPS OF STEAK AND SMOTHER WITH GRAVY.

NOTES

COTTAGE PIE

INGREDIENTS:

- 1 CLOVE - DICED GARLIC   ⎫
- ½ CUP - DICED ONIONS   ⎬ G.O.P.
- ½ CUP - DICED PEPPERS   ⎭
- 2 PACKAGES - RAMEN NOODLES
- 3 CUPS - WATER
- ½ LB. - GROUND BEEF
- 1 BOX - INSTANT GARLIC MASHED POTATOES
- 1 CAN - CORN, DRAINED
- ½ CUP - CHEDDAR CHEESE
- 1 TABLESPOON - EXTRA VIRGIN OLIVE OIL
- SEASON ALL - TO TASTE

DIRECTIONS:

1. IN A LARGE FRYING PAN COOK THE G.O.P. WITH OLIVE OIL UNTIL BROWNED.

2. ADD GROUND BEEF TO THE PAN WITH THE G.O.P ALONG WITH SEASON ALL.

PREPARE THE MASHED POTATOES ACCORDING TO PRODUCT INSTRUCTIONS.

3. IN ANOTHER POT ADD 3 CUPS OF WATER AND BRING TO BOIL. BREAK UP THE PACKAGES OF RAMEN AND ADD TO THE BOILING WATER

4. COOK THE NOODLES UNTIL TENDER BUT STILL FIRM, STIRRING ONCE OR TWICE TO BREAK APART. DRAIN WELL.

5. NEXT GREASE A PAN AND PLACE A FIRST LAYER OF THE NOODLES,

6. THEN ADD A LAYER OF THE GROUND BEEF AND G.O.P. MIXTURE

7. ADD A LAYER OF CHEESE AND CORN

8. TOP THAT WITH MASHED POTATOES AND ANOTHER LAYER OF CHEESE

9. THEN BAKE IN AN OVEN AT 350° FOR 10 MIN. OR UNTIL THE CHEESE IS MELTED OR BROWNED.

NOTES

RAMEN N' POT ROAST

INGREDIENTS:

- 1 CLOVE - DICED GARLIC } G.O.P.
- ½ CUP - DICED ONIONS
- ½ CUP - DICED PEPPERS
- 2 PACKAGES - RAMEN NOODLES
- 3 CUPS - WATER
- A SMALL ROAST
- ½ CUP - CARROTS
- 1 TABLESPOON - DRIED BASIL LEAVES
- 1 TABLESPOON - DRIED SCALLIONS
- 1 CAN OF BEEF BROTH
- ½ CUP CORN
- 1 POTATO - DICED
- ½ CUP - GREEN BEANS
- 1 TABLESPOON - EXTRA VIRGIN OLIVE OIL
- STEAK SEASONING - TO TASTE
- 1 TABLE SPOON - SOY SAUCE
- ¼ CUP - RED WINE

DIRECTIONS:

1. CUT SLITS INTO ROAST ADD A BASIL, GARLIC, SCALLIONS AND OLIVE OIL MIXTURE INTO THEM

2. LET THAT MARINATE IN SOME RED WINE FOR 24HRS (1HR. MINIMUM)

3. IN A LARGE FRYING PAN COOK THE G.O.P. WITH OLIVE OIL UNTIL BROWNED AND SET INTO THE SLOW COOKER.

4. ADD THE ROAST ALONG WITH THE CORN, CARROTS, GREEN BEANS AND BROTH TO A SLOW COOKER ON LOW HEAT FOR 8 HOURS

5. IN ANOTHER POT ADD 3 CUPS OF WATER AND BRING TO BOIL. BREAK UP THE PACKAGES OF RAMEN AND ADD TO THE BOILING WATER

6. COOK THE NOODLES UNTIL TENDER BUT STILL FIRM, STIRRING ONCE OR TWICE TO BREAK APART. DRAIN WELL,

7. SET A BED OF NOODLES ON A PLATE THEN TOP WITH SLICES OF THE BEEF ROAST. THEN DRIZZLE SOME JUICES OF FROM THE ROAST ON TOP.

NOTES

GLAZED STEAK AND VEGGIE NOODLES

INGREDIENTS:

* 1 CLOVE - DICED GARLIC
* ½ CUP - DICED ONIONS   } G.O.P.
* ½ CUP - DICED PEPPERS
* 2 PACKAGES - RAMEN NOODLES
* 2 CUPS - WATER
* 1/2 LB. - STEAK STRIPS
* 1 TABLESPOON - EXTRA VIRGIN OLIVE OIL
* STEAK SEASONING - TO TASTE
* ½ A BAG - FROZEN MIXED VEGETABLES
* 1 TABLESPOON - SOY SAUCE
* ½ CUP - PEACH-APRICOT MARMALADE
* 3 TABLESPOONS - TERYAKI MARINADE

DIRECTIONS:

1. IN A LARGE FRYING PAN COOK THE G.O.P. WITH OLIVE OIL UNTIL BROWNED

2. ADD SLICES OF STEAK TO THE PAN WITH THE G.O.P. ALONG WITH STEAK SEASONING , TERYAKI MARINADE. AND SOY SAUCE.

3. IN ANOTHER POT ADD 3 CUPS OF WATER AND BRING TO BOIL. BREAK UP THE PACKAGES OF RAMEN AND ADD TO THE BOILING WATER

4. ONCE THE STEAK IS COOKED, ADD THE MIXED VEGETABLES AND COOK UNTIL HOT AND STILL CRISP

5. COOK THE NOODLES UNTIL TENDER BUT STILL FIRM, STIRRING ONCE OR TWICE TO BREAK APART. DRAIN WELL, THEN SET THEM BACK INTO THE POT AND MIX IN THE MARMALADE OVER A LOW HEAT UNTIL THE NOODLES ARE COATED.

6. SET A BED OF NOODLES ON A PLATE THEN TOP BEEF AND MIXED VEGETABLES.

B'10

Oodles of Options

Pork Recipes

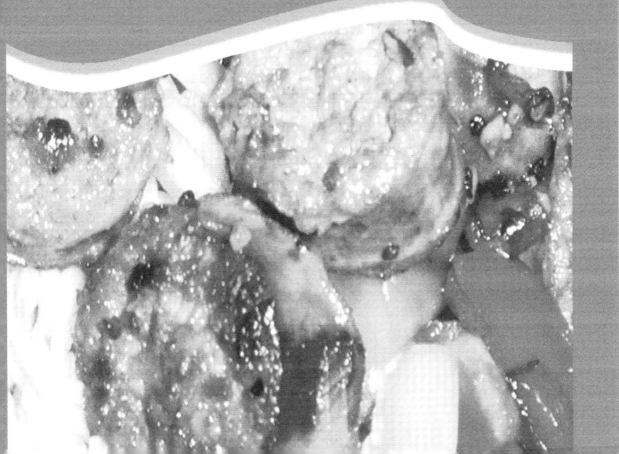

NOTES

HAM AND CHEESE

INGREDIENTS:

- 1 CLOVE - DICED GARLIC ⎫
- ½ CUP - DICED ONIONS   ⎬ G.O.P.
- ½ CUP - DICED PEPPERS   ⎭
- 2 PACKAGES - RAMEN NOODLES
- 3 CUPS - OF WATER
- 8 OZ - SLICED HAM
- 4 SLICES - AMERICAN AND CHEDDAR CHEESE
- ¼ CUP - MILK
- 1 TABLESPOON - EXTRA VIRGIN OLIVE OIL
- 1 CUP - SHREDDED LETTUCE
- 1/2 CUP - DICED TOMATOES

DIRECTIONS:

1. IN A LARGE FRYING PAN COOK THE G.O.P. WITH OLIVE OIL UNTIL BROWNED

2. ADD HAM TO THE PAN WITH THE G.O.P. AND SAUTÉ UNTIL BROWNED.

3. IN ANOTHER POT ADD 3 CUPS OF WATER AND BRING TO BOIL. BREAK UP THE PACKAGES OF RAMEN AND ADD TO THE BOILING WATER

4. COOK THE NOODLES UNTIL TENDER BUT STILL FIRM, STIRRING ONCE OR TWICE TO BREAK APART. DRAIN WELL.

5. NEXT ADD THEM TO THE PAN WITH THE HAM ALONG WITH THE CHEESE AND THE MILK, AND STIR UNTIL CREAMY.

6. SERVE ON TOP OF A BED OF LETTUCE AND TOMATOES OR AS IS.

NOTES

ROAST PORK & RAMEN

INGREDIENTS:

- 1 CLOVE - DICED GARLIC   ⎫
- ½ CUP - DICED ONIONS   ⎬ G.O.P.
- ½ CUP - DICED PEPPERS   ⎭
- 1 PACKAGE - RAMEN NOODLES
- 2-3 LB. - RUMP ROAST
- ¼ CUP - CARROTS
- 2 DRIED - BAY LEAVES
- 1 TEASPOON - ROSEMARY
- 1 TEASPOON - BASIL
- 1 TEASPOON - OREGANO
- 1 TEASPOON - CUMIN
- 1 TEASPOON - OLIVES DICED)
- 1 TEASPOON - LEMON JUICE
- 1 TABLESPOON - EXTRA VIRGIN OLIVE OIL
- SEASON ALL- TO TASTE
- ½ CUP - COOKING WINE
- 3 TEASPOONS - BALSAMIC VINAIGRETTE

DIRECTIONS:

1. CUT SLITS INTO ROAST ADD THE BASIL, GARLIC, ROSEMARY, DICED ONIONS, CUMIN AND OLIVES, AND OIL MIXTURE INTO IT.

2. LET THAT MARINATE IN SOME WHITE COOKING WINE AND LEMON JUICE.

3. AFTER 24 HOURS OF MARINATING(1 HR MIN) PLACE IN THE OVEN FOR A FEW HOURS AT 350 DEGREES.

4. IN A LARGE FRYING PAN COOK THE G.O.P. WITH OLIVE OIL UNTIL BROWNED

5. BREAK UP THE RAMEN NOODLES AND ADD THEM TO THE G.O.P. MIXTURE DRY AND ADD THE CARROTS AND THE BALSAMIC VINAIGRETTE

6. ONCE THE NOODLES AND CARROTS HAVE BROWNED SET THEM TO THE SIDE

7. ON A SERVING PLATE SET SLICES PORK ROAST. THEN SPRINKLE THE NOODLES, CARROTS AND G.O.P. OVER TOP AS A GARNISH AND DRIZZLE SOME GRAVY FROM THE ROAST ON TOP.

NOTES

HAM BBQ

INGREDIENTS:

- 1 CLOVE - DICED GARLIC
- ½ CUP - DICED ONIONS } G.O.P.
- ½ CUP - DICED PEPPERS
- 2 PACKAGES - RAMEN NOODLES (BROKEN INTO SMALL PIECES)
- 3 CUPS - WATER
- 8 OZ.- CHIPPED HAM
- ½ CUP - BBQ SAUCE
- 1 TABLESPOON - EXTRA VIRGIN OLIVE OIL
- CRACKERS OR SMALL BUNS

DIRECTIONS:

1. IN A LARGE FRYING PAN COOK THE G.O.P. WITH OLIVE OIL UNTIL BROWNED

2. ADD HAM TO THE PAN WITH THE G.O.P. AND SAUTÉ UNTIL BROWNED.

3. IN ANOTHER POT ADD 3 CUPS OF WATER AND BRING TO BOIL. BREAK UP THE PACKAGES OF RAMEN AND ADD TO THE BOILING WATER

4. COOK THE NOODLES UNTIL TENDER BUT STILL FIRM, STIRRING ONCE OR TWICE TO BREAK APART. DRAIN WELL,

5. NEXT ADD THEM TO THE PAN WITH THE HAM ALONG WITH THE BBQ SAUCE AND MIX.

6. CONTINUE TO MIX UNTIL THE HAM AND NOODLES ARE COMPLETELY COVERED

7. SERVE ON A BUN OR ON A PLATE WITH CRACKERS AND CHEESE

NOTES

SAUSAGE & PEPPERS

INGREDIENTS:

- 1 CLOVE - DICED GARLIC
- ½ CUP - DICED RED ONIONS   } G.O.P.
- ½ CUP - DICED PEPPERS
  (USE YELLOW, RED, AND GREEN BELL PEPPERS)
- 2 PACKAGES - RAMEN NOODLES
- 2 CUPS - WATER
- 8 OZ. - ITALIAN SAUSAGE LINKS (SLICED)
- 1 TABLESPOON - EXTRA VIRGIN OLIVE OIL
- ¼ CUP - GRATED ROMANO OR PARMESAN CHEESE

DIRECTIONS:

1. IN A LARGE FRYING PAN COOK THE G.O.P. WITH OLIVE OIL
   UNTIL BROWNED

2. ADD SAUSAGE TO THE PAN WITH THE G.O.P. AND SAUTÉ UNTIL BROWNED.
   THEN DRAIN THE FAT.

3. IN ANOTHER POT ADD 3 CUPS OF WATER AND BRING TO BOIL. BREAK
   UP THE PACKAGES OF RAMEN AND ADD TO THE BOILING WATER.

4. COOK THE NOODLES UNTIL TENDER BUT STILL FIRM, STIRRING ONCE
   OR TWICE TO BREAK APART. DRAIN WELL,

5. NEXT ADD THEM TO THE PAN WITH THE SAUSAGE AND MIX UNTIL
   THE NOODLES ARE BROWNED

6. SERVE ON A PLATE AND SPRINKLE CHEESE OVER THE TOP.

NOTES

PORK LO MEIN

INGREDIENTS:

- 1 CLOVE - DICED GARLIC
- ½ CUP - DICED ONIONS   } G.O.P.
- ½ CUP - DICED PEPPERS
- 2 PACKAGES - RAMEN NOODLES
- 2 CUPS - WATER
- 2 PORK CUTLETS - SLICED INTO 1/2 IN STRIPS
- 1 TABLESPOON - EXTRA VIRGIN OLIVE OIL
- SEASON ALL-TO TASTE
- ½ A BAG OF FROZEN STIR-FRY VEGETABLES
- 2 TABLE SPOONS - SOY SAUCE

DIRECTIONS:

1. IN A LARGE FRYING PAN COOK THE G.O.P. WITH OLIVE OIL UNTIL BROWNED

2. ADD SLICES OF PORK TO THE PAN WITH THE G.O.P. ALONG WITH SEASON ALL AND THE SOY SAUCE.

3. IN ANOTHER POT ADD 3 CUPS OF WATER AND BRING TO BOIL. BREAK UP THE PACKAGES OF RAMEN AND ADD TO THE BOILING WATER

4. COOK THE NOODLES UNTIL TENDER BUT STILL FIRM, STIRRING ONCE OR TWICE TO BREAK APART. DRAIN WELL,

5. ONCE THE PORK IS COOKED ADD THE MIXED VEGETABLES AND THE NOODLES AND COOK UNTIL THE VEGETABLES ARE HOT AND STILL CRISP.

6. THEN IT IS READY TO SERVE!!

NOTES

BACON EGG AND CHEESE OMELET

INGREDIENTS:

- 1 CLOVE - DICED GARLIC
- ½ CUP - DICED ONIONS   } G.O.P.
- ½ CUP - DICED PEPPERS
- 2 PACKAGES - RAMEN NOODLES
- 3 CUPS - WATER
- 4 SLICES - BACON
- 3 LARGE - EGGS
- 2 SLICES - AMERICAN CHEESE
- 1 TABLESPOON - EXTRA VIRGIN OLIVE OIL
- SALT AND PEPPER TO TASTE
- ½ CUP - SLICED MUSHROOMS

DIRECTIONS:

1. IN A LARGE PAN SAUTÉ G.O.P. AND MUSHROOMS WITH OLIVE OIL UNTIL BROWNED, THEN SET THEM ON A PLATE TO THE SIDE.

2. PLACE THE EGGS IN A BOWL AND WHISK UNTIL THE YOLKS MIX THE WHITES ADD SOME SALT AN PEPPER TO IT.

3. PLACE THE STRIPS OF BACON INTO THE PAN AND COOK UNTIL BROWNED AND CRISPY.

4. IN ANOTHER POT ADD 3 CUPS OF WATER AND BRING TO BOIL. BREAK UP THE PACKAGES OF RAMEN AND ADD TO THE BOILING WATER

5. ONCE THE BACON IS COOKED SET IT TO THE SIDE WITH THE VEGETABLES

6. TAKE THE EGGS AND PUT THEM INTO THE OILED PAN AND COOK UNTIL THICKENED

7. ONCE THE EGGS ARE FINISHED ADD THE BACON AND VEGETABLES AND SLICES OF CHEESE TO ONE SIDE AND FLIP THE OTHER SIDE OVER THE TOP.

8. COOK THE NOODLES UNTIL TENDER BUT STILL FIRM, STIRRING ONCE OR TWICE TO BREAK APART. DRAIN WELL, THEN MELT SOME CHEESE OVER THE TOP AND MIX UNTIL CREAMY.

9. SET A BED OF CHEESY NOODLES ON A PLATE THEN TOP WITH THE OMELET

NOTES

CHOPS & NOODLES

INGREDIENTS:

- 1 CLOVE - DICED GARLIC } G.O.P.
- ½ CUP - DICED ONIONS
- ½ CUP - DICED PEPPERS
- 2 PACKAGES - RAMEN NOODLES
- 3 CUPS - WATER
- 2 - PORK CHOPS
- 1 TABLESPOON - EXTRA VIRGIN OLIVE OIL
- SEASON ALL TO TASTE
- ½ A BAG OF FROZEN GREEN BEANS
- LEMON PEPPER SEASONING TO TASTE
- 1 TABLESPOON DRIED PARSLEY

DIRECTIONS:

1. IN A LARGE FRYING PAN COOK THE G.O.P. WITH OLIVE OIL UNTIL BROWNED

2. ADD PORK CHOPS TO THE PAN WITH THE G.O.P ALONG WITH SEASON ALL AND LEMON PEPPER SEASONING.

3. IN ANOTHER POT ADD 3 CUPS OF WATER AND BRING TO BOIL. BREAK UP THE PACKAGES OF RAMEN AND ADD TO THE BOILING WATER

4. COOK THE NOODLES UNTIL TENDER BUT STILL FIRM, STIRRING ONCE OR TWICE TO BREAK APART. DRAIN WELL,

5. ADD THE PARSLEY ALONG WITH OIL AND THE NOODLES TO THE POT AND MIX WELL.

6. ONCE THE PORK CHOPS ARE COOKED ADD THE GREEN BEANS AND COOK UNTIL THE VEGETABLES ARE HOT BUT STILL CRISP.

7. SET A BED OF NOODLES ON A PLATE THEN TOP WITH PORK AND GREEN BEANS.

NOTES

LATIN PORK CHOPS

INGREDIENTS:

- 1 CLOVE – DICED GARLIC
- ½ CUP – DICED ONIONS   } G.O.P.
- ½ CUP – DICED PEPPERS
- 2 PACKAGES – RAMEN NOODLES
- 3 CUPS – WATER
- PORK CHOPS
- 2 TABLESPOONS – OLIVE OIL
- 3 TABLESPOONS – SOFRITO
- ½ CAN – TOMATO SAUCE
- SEASON ALL TO TASTE
- GARLIC POWDER
- ONION POWDER
- 1/4 CUP – VINEGAR

DIRECTIONS:

1. MARINATE THE PORK CHOPS WITH GARLIC AND ONION POWDER AND SEASON ALL AND VINEGAR FOR AT LEAST ONE HOUR

2. IN A LARGE FRYING PAN SAUTÉ THE PORK CHOPS IN OIL . THEN ADD THE G.O.P.

3. SAUTÉ G.O.P. IN THE PAN WITH PORK CHOPS UNTIL BROWNED WELL ON BOTH SIDES

4. IN ANOTHER POT ADD 3 CUPS OF WATER AND BRING TO BOIL. BREAK UP THE PACKAGES OF RAMEN AND ADD TO THE BOILING WATER

5. COOK THE NOODLES UNTIL TENDER BUT STILL FIRM, STIRRING ONCE OR TWICE TO BREAK APART. DRAIN WELL, PLACE THEM BACK IN THE POT. ADD THE TOMATO SAUCE, AND SOFRITO AND MIX WELL UNTIL DONE.

6. SET A BED OF NOODLES ON A PLATE THEN TOP WITH THE PORK CHOPS.

NOTES

NOODLE STUFFING

INGREDIENTS:

- 1 CLOVE - DICED GARLIC } G.O.P.
- ½ CUP - DICED ONIONS
- ½ CUP - DICED PEPPERS
- 2 PACKAGES - RAMEN NOODLES
- 3 CUPS - WATER
- 8 OZ - SAGE SEASONED SAUSAGE
- 1 TABLESPOON - EXTRA VIRGIN OLIVE OIL
- 1 CUP - CELERY
- POULTRY SEASONING- TO TASTE
- 1 CUP - ITALIAN SEASONED BREAD CRUMBS
- 1 CUP - CHICKEN BROTH

DIRECTIONS:

1. IN A LARGE PAN SAUTÉ G.O.P. AND SAUSAGE IN PAN WITH OLIVE OIL UNTIL BROWNED

2. BREAK UP THE DRIED NOODLES AND ADD THEM INTO A BOWL ALONG WITH THE BREAD CRUMBS

3. ADD THE GOP AND SAUSAGE TO THE BOWL AND POUR IN THE CHICKEN BROTH AND MIX IN WITH THE POULTRY SEASONING.

4. SET THE MIXTURE INTO A BAKING PAN AND BAKE AT 350 DEGREES IN THE OVEN UNTIL BROWNED AND CRISPY ON TOP.

NOTES

CUBAN NOODLES

INGREDIENTS:

- 1 CLOVE - DICED GARLIC ⎫
- ½ CUP - DICED ONIONS   ⎬ G.O.P.
- ½ CUP - DICED PEPPERS ⎭
- 2 PACKAGES - RAMEN NOODLES
- 3 CUPS - WATER
- 4 OZ - SLICED ROAST PORK (SEE RECIPE P2)
- 4 OZ - SLICED HAM
- 1 TABLESPOON - EXTRA VIRGIN OLIVE OIL
- 2 TABLESPOONS - DELI BROWN MUSTARD
- SLICES OF ANY SOFT WHITE CHEESE OR SWISS CHEESE
- SLICED DILL PICKLES

DIRECTIONS:

1. IN A POT ADD 3 CUPS OF WATER AND BRING TO BOIL. BREAK UP THE PACKAGES OF RAMEN AND ADD TO THE BOILING WATER

2. COOK THE NOODLES UNTIL TENDER BUT STILL FIRM, STIRRING ONCE OR TWICE TO BREAK APART. DRAIN WELL, PLACE THEM BACK IN THE POT AND ADD THE G.O.P.

3. SAUTÉ G.O.P AND NOODLES IN PAN WITH OLIVE OIL UNTIL BROWNED THEN MIX IN THE MUSTARD.

4. THEN ADD THE ROAST PORK (SEE P2) AND THE HAM AND BROWN ON ALL SIDES.

5. PLACE ALL THE MIXTURE ONTO A PLATE THEN TOP WITH SLICES OF CHEESE AND PICKLES.

Oodles of Options

Veggie Recipes

NOTES

PASTA SALAD

INGREDIENTS:

- 1 CLOVE - DICED GARLIC
- ½ CUP - DICED ONIONS   } G.O.P.
- ½ CUP - DICED PEPPERS
- 2 PACKAGES - RAMEN NOODLES
- 3 CUPS - WATER
- 1 TABLE SPOON - EXTRA VIRGIN OLIVE OIL OR MAYONNAISE
- 1 CUP - DICED CELERY
- 1 CUP - CHEDDAR CHEESE CUBES
- ½ CUP - BROCCOLI
- ½ CUP - SLICED CARROTS
- ¼ CUP - SUN DRIED TOMATOES DICED
- ¼ CUP - SLICED BLACK OLIVES

DIRECTIONS:

1. IN A POT ADD 3 CUPS OF WATER AND BRING TO BOIL. BREAK UP THE PACKAGES OF RAMEN AND ADD TO THE BOILING WATER

2. COOK THE NOODLES UNTIL TENDER BUT STILL FIRM, STIRRING ONCE OR TWICE TO BREAK APART. DRAIN WELL, THEN SET THEM A BOWL

3. ADD THE GOP MIXTURE ALONG WITH THE BLACK OLIVES, SUN DRIED TOMATOES, CARROTS, SLICED BROCCOLI, CELERY AND CHEDDAR CHEESE CUBES

4. POUR IN OLIVE OIL OR MAYONNAISE AND MIX WITH ALL THE INGREDIENTS UNTIL COATED

NOTES

GREEN GODDESS SALAD

INGREDIENTS:

- 1 CLOVE - DICED GARLIC
- ½ CUP - DICED ONIONS
- ½ CUP - DICED PEPPERS

} G.O.P.

- 2 PACKAGES - RAMEN NOODLES
- 3 CUPS - WATER
- ½ CUP - DICED CELERY
- ½ CUP - GREEN GODDESS SALAD DRESSING
- ½ CUP - BROCCOLI
- ½ CUP - SLICED OLIVES
- ½ CUP - PEAS
- ½ CUP - GREEN BEANS
- 1 - AVOCADO DICED

DIRECTIONS:

1. IN POT ADD 3 CUPS OF WATER AND BRING TO BOIL. BREAK UP THE PACKAGES OF RAMEN AND ADD TO THE BOILING WATER

2. COOK THE NOODLES UNTIL TENDER BUT STILL FIRM, STIRRING ONCE OR TWICE TO BREAK APART. DRAIN WELL, AND SET IN A BOWL.

3. ADD THE GOP MIXTURE ALONG WITH THE OLIVES, AVOCADO, PEAS, GREEN BEANS, SLICED BROCCOLI, AND CELERY

4. POUR IN AND GREEN GODDESS DRESSING AND MIX WELL UNTIL COATED THOROUGHLY.

NOTES

EGGPLANT PARMESAN

INGREDIENTS:

- 1 CLOVE - DICED GARLIC
- ½ CUP - DICED ONIONS   } G.O.P.
- ½ CUP - DICED PEPPERS
- 2 PACKAGES - RAMEN NOODLES
- 3 CUPS - WATER
- 2 SLICED - EGGPLANTS
- 2 CUPS - MOZZARELLA AND PARMESAN CHEESE (1 CUP EACH)
- 1 TABLESPOON - EXTRA VIRGIN OLIVE OIL
- 1 24 OZ BOTTLE. - TOMATO SAUCE
- 1 CUP - MUSHROOMS

DIRECTIONS:

1. SAUTÉ G.O.P. AND MUSHROOMS IN PAN WITH OLIVE OIL UNTIL BROWNED THEN ADD THE TOMATO SAUCE MIX TOGETHER OVER A MEDIUM HEAT, THEN REDUCE TO A SIMMER

2. IN ANOTHER POT ADD 3 CUPS OF WATER AND BRING TO BOIL. BREAK UP THE PACKAGES OF RAMEN AND ADD TO THE BOILING WATER

3. COOK THE NOODLES UNTIL TENDER BUT STILL FIRM, STIRRING ONCE OR TWICE TO BREAK APART. DRAIN WELL,

4. IN A GREASED 13 X 9 BAKING PAN LAYER THE NOODLES, CHEESE, EGGPLANT AND SAUCE ALTERNATING AS YOU WOULD A LASAGNA

5. TOP THE LAST LAYER WITH A GOOD COVER OF SAUCE AND CHEESE THEN BAKE IN THE OVEN AT 350° UNTIL CHEESE IS MELTED AND BROWNED. AND THE CASSEROLE IS HEATED THROUGH.

V3

NOTES

PORTABELLA MUSHROOM NOODLES

INGREDIENTS:

- 1 CLOVE - DICED GARLIC
- ½ CUP - DICED ONIONS   } G.O.P.
- ½ CUP - DICED PEPPERS
- 2 PACKAGES - RAMEN NOODLES
- 3 CUPS - WATER
- 1 TABLESPOON - EXTRA VIRGIN OLIVE OIL
- 3 LARGE - PORTABELLA MUSHROOMS
- SOY SAUCE - TO TASTE
- WORCESTERSHIRE SAUCE - TO TASTE
- ½ CUP - BALSAMIC VINEGAR
- ¼ CUP - BLACK OLIVES
- 2 CUPS - SPRING SALAD MIX
- STEAK SEASONING TO TASTE

DIRECTIONS:

1. COAT THE PORTABELLA MUSHROOMS IN SOME SOY SAUCE, THE BALSAMIC VINEGAR AND WORCESTERSHIRE SAUCE

2. SAUTÉ G.O.P. IN PAN WITH OLIVE OIL UNTIL BROWNED THEN SET ASIDE

3. SLICE UP THE PORTABELLA MUSHROOMS AND ADD THE STEAK SEASONING, THESE CAN BE GREAT IF PLACED ON A GRILL OR COOKED IN A PAN.

4. IN ANOTHER POT ADD 3 CUPS OF WATER AND BRING TO BOIL. BREAK UP THE PACKAGES OF RAMEN AND ADD TO THE BOILING WATER

5. COOK THE NOODLES UNTIL TENDER BUT STILL FIRM, STIRRING ONCE OR TWICE TO BREAK APART. THEN ADD THEM TO THE GOP MIXTURE AND OIL AND SAUTÉ WITH THE MUSHROOMS AND THE OLIVES

6. SET A BED OF THE SPRING MIX ON A PLATE TOP WITH THE SEASONED NOODLES, MUSHROOMS AND OLIVES

NOTES

STUFFED PEPPERS

INGREDIENTS:

- 1 CLOVE - DICED GARLIC ⎫
- ½ CUP - DICED ONIONS ⎬ G.O.P.
- ½ CUP - DICED PEPPERS ⎭
- 2 PACKAGES - RAMEN NOODLES
- 3 CUPS - WATER
- 4 - BELL PEPPERS, CORED AND SEEDED FOR STUFFING
- 6 - VEGGIE SAUSAGE PATTIES, CHOPPED INTO CUBES
- 1 TABLESPOON - EXTRA VIRGIN OLIVE OIL
- ¼ CUP - FRESH BASIL
- 1 TEASPOON - OREGANO, DRIED
- ½ CUP - CELERY, DICED
- 1 CUP - TOMATO SAUCE
- SEASON ALL TO TASTE

DIRECTIONS:

1. SAUTÉ G.O.P. AND CHOPPED UP SAUSAGE IN A PAN WITH OLIVE OIL UNTIL BROWNED THEN SET THEM ON A PLATE

2. IN ANOTHER POT ADD 3 CUPS OF WATER AND BRING TO BOIL. BREAK UP THE PACKAGES OF RAMEN AND ADD TO THE BOILING WATER

3. COOK THE NOODLES UNTIL TENDER BUT STILL FIRM, STIRRING ONCE OR TWICE TO BREAK APART. DRAIN WELL, THEN ADD THE GOP AND SAUSAGE MIXTURE AND OIL TOGETHER AND CONTINUE TO SAUTÉ.

4. ADD 1 CUP OF TOMATO SAUCE AND BASIL AND CELERY TO MIXTURE AND SIMMER

5. ONCE FINISHED SPOON THE MIXTURE INTO THE PEPPERS

6. SET IN A GREASED PAN. BAKE IN THE OVEN ON 350 FOR 20 MIN

NOTES

TOMATO AND BASIL SALAD

INGREDIENTS:

- 1 CLOVE - DICED GARLIC ⎫
- ½ CUP - DICED ONIONS   ⎬ G.O.P.
- ½ CUP - DICED PEPPERS ⎭
- 2 PACKAGES - RAMEN NOODLES
- 3 CUPS - WATER
- 1 CUP - FRESH MOZZARELLA CHEESE, SLICED
- 1 TABLESPOON - EXTRA VIRGIN OLIVE OIL
- ½ CUP FRESH BASIL LEAVES, CHOPPED
- 2 CUPS - SPRING SALAD MIX
- 2 - DICED TOMATOES
- 3 TABLESPOONS - BASIL PESTO

DIRECTIONS:

1. IN A POT ADD 3 CUPS OF WATER AND BRING TO BOIL. BREAK UP THE PACKAGES OF RAMEN AND ADD TO THE BOILING WATER

2. COOK THE NOODLES UNTIL TENDER BUT STILL FIRM, STIRRING ONCE OR TWICE TO BREAK APART. DRAIN WELL

3. SAUTÉ G.O.P. IN PAN WITH OLIVE OIL UNTIL BROWNED THEN SET THEM ON A PLATE TO THE SIDE.

4. SLICE UP THE MOZZARELLA, TOMATOES, AND BASIL

5. ADD THE DRAINED NOODLES AND PESTO TO THE GOP MIXTURE AND CONTINUE TO SAUTE'

6. SET A BED OF THE SPRING MIX ON A PLATE TOP WITH THE SEASONED NOODLES

7. THEN TOP THE SALAD WITH TOMATOES, BASIL, AND MOZZARELLA CHEESE

NOTES

HASH BROWN NOODLES

INGREDIENTS:

- 1 CLOVE - DICED GARLIC   ⎫
- ½ CUP - DICED ONIONS   ⎬ G.O.P.
- ½ CUP - DICED PEPPERS   ⎭
- 2 PACKAGES - RAMEN NOODLES
- 3 CUPS - WATER
- 1 CUP CHEDDAR CHEESE
- 1 TABLESPOON EXTRA VIRGIN OLIVE OIL
- 1 CUP POTATOES CUT INTO CUBES
- 2 TABLESPOONS ITALIAN SEASONING
- SEASON ALL TO TASTE

DIRECTIONS:

1. SAUTÉ G.O.P. IN PAN WITH OLIVE OIL UNTIL BROWNED THEN SET THEM ON A PLATE TO THE SIDE.

2. IN ANOTHER POT ADD THE WATER AND BRING TO A BOIL AND COOK THE POTATOES UNTIL SOFTENED, THEN DRAIN AND SET TO THE SIDE.

3. ADD MORE WATER TO THE POT AND THEN BRING TO BOIL AND BREAK UP THE PACKAGES OF RAMEN AND ADD TO THE BOILING WATER

4. COOK THE NOODLES UNTIL TENDER BUT STILL FIRM, STIRRING ONCE OR TWICE TO BREAK APART. DRAIN WELL,

5. THEN ADD THE DRAINED NOODLES AND POTATOES TO GOP MIXTURE AND SAUTÉ UNTIL BROWNED.

6. TOP WITH THE CHEDDAR CHEESE AND SERVE UP WITH YOUR FAVORITE BREAKFAST DISHES.

NOTES

HEARTY NOODLE OMELET

INGREDIENTS:

- 1 CLOVE - DICED GARLIC   ⎫
- ½ CUP - DICED ONIONS   ⎬ G.O.P.
- ½ CUP - DICED PEPPERS   ⎭
- 2 PACKAGES - RAMEN NOODLES
- 3 CUPS - WATER
- 2 - ¼ CUP - BLUE CHEESE, CRUMBLED
- 1 TABLESPOON - EXTRA VIRGIN OLIVE OIL
- SALT AND PEPPER TO TASTE
- ½ CUP - MUSHROOMS
- 4 - LARGE EGGS

DIRECTIONS:

1. SAUTÉ G.O.P. AND MUSHROOMS IN PAN WITH OLIVE OIL UNTIL BROWNED THEN SET ASIDE.

2. PLACE THE EGGS IN A BOWL AND WHISK UNTIL THE YOLKS MIX THE WHITES ADD SOME SALT AN PEPPER TO IT.

3. IN ANOTHER POT ADD 3 CUPS OF WATER AND BRING TO BOIL. BREAK UP THE PACKAGES OF RAMEN AND ADD TO THE BOILING WATER. COOK THE NOODLES UNTIL TENDER BUT STILL FIRM, STIRRING ONCE OR TWICE TO BREAK APART. DRAIN WELL.

4. ONCE THE NOODLES ARE FINISHED AND DRAINED, PLACE THEM IN THE POT WITH THE GOP MIXTURE AND MELT THE 1ST 1/4 CUP OF CHEESE OVER THE TOP.

5. TAKE THE EGGS AND PUT THEM INTO THE OILED PAN AND COOK UNTIL THICKENED

6. ONCE THE EGGS ARE FINISHED ADD THE VEGETABLE AND CRUMBLED CHEESE TO ONE SIDE AND FLIP THE OTHER SIDE OVER THE TOP.

7. SET A BED OF CHEESY NOODLES ON A PLATE THEN TOP WITH THE OMELET

NOTES

VEGGIE STIR FRY

INGREDIENTS:

- 1 CLOVE - DICED GARLIC
- ½ CUP - DICED ONIONS   } G.O.P.
- ½ CUP - DICED PEPPERS
- 2 PACKAGES - RAMEN NOODLES
- 3 CUPS - WATER
- 1 BAG - FROZEN ASIAN MIXED VEGGIES, THAWED
- 1 TABLESPOON - EXTRA VIRGIN OLIVE OIL
- ¼ CUP - SOY SAUCE
- ¼ CUP - DUCK SAUCE (TO ADD SOME SWEETNESS)*

DIRECTIONS:

1. SAUTÉ G.O.P. IN LARGE PAN WITH OLIVE OIL UNTIL BROWNED.

2. ADD MIXED VEGETABLES TO THE PAN WITH THE G.O.P. AND SAUTÉ UNTIL BROWNED.

3. IN ANOTHER POT ADD 3 CUPS OF WATER AND BRING TO BOIL. BREAK UP THE PACKAGES OF RAMEN AND ADD TO THE BOILING WATER

4. COOK THE NOODLES UNTIL TENDER BUT STILL FIRM, STIRRING ONCE OR TWICE TO BREAK APART. DRAIN WELL,

5. ADD THE NOODLES TO THE PAN WITH THE VEGGIE MIXTURE AND THOROUGHLY COAT WITH SOY SAUCE AND OR DUCK SAUCE

*ANOTHER OPTION FOR SAUCE IS IF THE MIXED VEGETABLES ALREADY COME WITH A SAUCE PACKET.

NOTES

GREEK SALAD

INGREDIENTS:

- 1 CLOVE - DICED GARLIC
- ½ CUP - DICED ONIONS
- ½ CUP - DICED PEPPERS

 } G.O.P.

- 2 PACKAGES - RAMEN NOODLES
- 3 CUPS - WATER
- ½ CUP - CRUMBLED FETA CHEESE
- 1 TABLESPOON - EXTRA VIRGIN OLIVE OIL
- ¼ CUP - BLACK OLIVES
- BALSAMIC VINEGAR - TO TASTE
- ½ CUP - FRESH BASIL
- 2 CUPS SPRING SALAD MIX
- 1 CUCUMBER , SLICED
- 1 TOMATO, DICED

DIRECTIONS:

1. SAUTÉ G.O.P. IN PAN WITH OLIVE OIL UNTIL BROWNED THEN SET THEM ON A PLATE TO THE SIDE.

2. SLICE UP THE CUCUMBERS, TOMATOES, OLIVES AND BASIL

3. IN ANOTHER POT ADD 3 CUPS OF WATER AND BRING TO BOIL. BREAK UP THE PACKAGES OF RAMEN AND ADD TO THE BOILING WATER

4. COOK THE NOODLES UNTIL TENDER BUT STILL FIRM, STIRRING ONCE OR TWICE TO BREAK APART. DRAIN WELL THEN ADD THE GOP MIXTURE AND OIL TOGETHER AND CONTINUE TO SAUTÉ

5. SET A BED OF THE SPRING MIX ON A PLATE TOP WITH THE SEASONED NOODLES AND THEN THE CUCUMBERS TOMATOES, OLIVES AND BASIL

6. THEN TOP THE SALAD WITH FETA CHEESE AND BALSAMIC VINEGAR

Oodles of Options

Seafood Recipes

NOTES

TUNA SALAD

INGREDIENTS:

- 1 CLOVE - DICED GARLIC
- ½ CUP - DICED ONIONS   } G.O.P.
- ½ CUP - DICED PEPPERS
- 2 PACKAGES - RAMEN NOODLES
- 3 CUPS - WATER
- 2 CANS - TUNA FISH IN WATER
- ½ CUP - DICED CELERY
- SEASON ALL OR SEAFOOD SEASONING - TO TASTE
- 2 - HARD BOILED EGGS SLICED
- 2 TABLESPOONS - OLIVE OIL OR MAYONNAISE

DIRECTIONS:

1. IN A LARGE BOWL, MIX THE CELERY , GARLIC, PEPPERS, ONIONS, AND EGG AND SET TO THE SIDE

2. IN ANOTHER POT ADD 3 CUPS OF WATER AND BRING TO BOIL. BREAK UP THE PACKAGES OF RAMEN AND ADD TO THE BOILING WATER

3. COOK THE NOODLES UNTIL TENDER BUT STILL FIRM, STIRRING ONCE OR TWICE TO BREAK APART. DRAIN WELL, ADD THEM TO THE BOWL AND STIR TOGETHER UNTIL NOODLES ARE COATED

4. ADD THE TUNA ALONG WITH THE OLIVE OIL OR MAYO TO THE BOWL AND MIX THOROUGHLY

5. SERVE THIS WARMED OR CHILLED

NOTES

CRAB CAKES

INGREDIENTS:

- 2 PACKAGES - RAMEN NOODLES
- 3 CUPS - WATER
- 8 OZ - CRAB MEAT
- OLD BAY OR CRAB SEASONING - TO TASTE
- 1 TABLESPOON -. WORCESTERSHIRE SAUCE
- 1 TEASPOON - SPICY MUSTARD
- 1 CUP - MILK
- 1 CUP - HEAVY CREME
- 1 CLOVE - DICED GARLIC
- ½ CUP - DICED ONIONS
- 3 - EGGS
- CANOLA OIL - FOR FRYING

DIRECTIONS:

1. IN A SMALL POT ADD 3 CUPS OF WATER AND BRING TO BOIL. BREAK UP THE PACKAGES OF RAMEN AND ADD TO THE BOILING WATER

2. COOK THE NOODLES UNTIL TENDER BUT STILL FIRM, STIRRING ONCE OR TWICE TO BREAK APART. DRAIN WELL, THEN SET THEM A BOWL AND ADD THE MILK FOR THE NOODLES TO SOAK UP.

3. HEAT UP THE CREAM TO A SIMMER, MAKE SURE IT DOES NOT BOIL

4. ADD THE GARLIC AND ONION ALONG WITH THE WORCESTERSHIRE SAUCE, SEAFOOD SEASONING AND THE NOODLES AND MIX WELL AND REFRIGERATE THE MIXTURE UNTIL STIFFENED.

5. IN A SMALL BOWL WHISK THE EGGS UNTIL THE YOLKS ARE MIXED TOGETHER. ONCE THE MIXTURE IS READY BEGIN TO FORM THEM INTO PATTIES BY ROLLING CRAB MEAT INTO BALLS AND THEN FLATTEN AND THEN DIP THEM INTO THE EGGS.

6. HEAT THE CANOLA OIL IN A FRYING PAN AND FRY THE PATTIES UNTIL THEY ARE BROWNED ON BOTH SIDES

NOTES

TUNA CASSEROLE

INGREDIENTS:

- 1 CLOVE – DICED GARLIC
- ½ CUP – DICED ONIONS   } G.O.P.
- ½ CUP – DICED PEPPERS
- 2 PACKAGES – RAMEN NOODLES
- 3 CUPS – WATER
- 2 CANS – TUNA
- ½ CUP – CELERY
- ½ CUP – PEAS
- 1 CAN – CREAM OF MUSHROOM SOUP
- SEASON ALL TO TASTE
- ITALIAN BREAD CRUMBS
- 2 TABLESPOONS OLIVE OIL OR MAYONNAISE

DIRECTIONS:

1. IN A LARGE BOWL CHOP UP THE CELERY , GARLIC, PEPPERS, ONIONS, AND PEAS .

2. ADD THE TUNA ALONG WITH THE OLIVE OIL OR MAYO AND THE CREAM OF MUSHROOM TO THE BOWL AND MIX THOROUGHLY

3. IN ANOTHER POT ADD 3 CUPS OF WATER AND BRING TO BOIL. BREAK UP THE PACKAGES OF RAMEN AND ADD TO THE BOILING WATER

4. COOK THE NOODLES UNTIL TENDER BUT STILL FIRM, STIRRING ONCE OR TWICE TO BREAK APART. DRAIN WELL, THEN BEGIN TO LAYER THEM IN AN A CASSEROLE DISH

5. ALTERNATE LAYERS OF NOODLES WITH THE MIXTURE FROM THE BOWL UNTIL YOU REACH THE TOP OF THE CASSEROLE DISH. APPROX. 4 LAYERS

6. WHEN THE LAYERS REACH THE TOP OF THE DISH SMOOTH THINGS OUT AND COVER WITH THE BREAD CRUMBS

7. BAKE THE CASSEROLE IN THE OVEN AT 350 FOR 30 MIN OR UNTIL THE TOP IS BROWNED AND THE CASSEROLE IS HEATED THROUGH

S3

NOTES

BBQ SHRIMP

INGREDIENTS:

- ✳ 1 CLOVE - DICED GARLIC
- ✳ ½ CUP - DICED ONIONS   } G.O.P.
- ✳ ½ CUP - DICED PEPPERS
- ✳ 2 PACKAGES - RAMEN NOODLES
- ✳ 8 OZ. - DEVEINED AND SHELLED SHRIMP
- ✳ SEASON ALL TO TASTE
- ✳ OLD BAY SEAFOOD SEASONING TO TASTE
- ✳ 3/4 CUP - BBQ SAUCE
- ✳ 2 TABLESPOONS SPICY BROWN MUSTARD
- ✳ 1 TABLESPOON OLIVE OIL

DIRECTIONS:

1. IN A LARGE PAN SAUTÉ G.O.P. IN PAN WITH OLIVE OIL UNTIL BROWNED.

2. ADD SHRIMP TO THE PAN WITH THE G.O.P ALONG WITH SEASON ALL*
   AND SEAFOOD SEASONING.

3. IN ANOTHER POT ADD 3 CUPS OF WATER AND BRING TO BOIL. BREAK
   UP THE PACKAGES OF RAMEN AND ADD TO THE BOILING WATER

4. COOK THE NOODLES UNTIL TENDER BUT STILL FIRM, STIRRING ONCE
   OR TWICE TO BREAK APART. DRAIN WELL, THEN ADD THEM TO THE
   PAN ALONG WITH THE BBQ SAUCE AND SPICY MUSTARD AND THE SHRIMP.

5. MIX ALL THE INGREDIENTS WELL UNTIL COATED

6. TO ADD THOSE AUTHENTIC BBQ FLAVORS WRAP THE INGREDIENTS IN
   FOIL AND COOK ON THE GRILL FOR 10 - 15 MINS..

NOTES

BAKED FISH IN RED SAUCE

INGREDIENTS:

- 1 CLOVE - DICED GARLIC
- ½ CUP - DICED ONIONS   } G.O.P.
- ½ CUP - DICED PEPPERS
- 2 PACKAGES - RAMEN NOODLES
- 3 CUPS - WATER
- 4 -6 - TALAPIA FILLETS
- 1 TABLESPOON - EXTRA VIRGIN OLIVE OIL
- ONE 8 OZ CAN - TOMATOES
- WHITE COOKING WINE
- SEAFOOD SEASONING TO TASTE
- 1 TABLESPOON - ITALIAN SEASONING

DIRECTIONS:

1. IN A LARGE PAN SAUTÉ G.O.P. IN PAN WITH OLIVE OIL UNTIL BROWNED.

2. MARINATE THE FISH WITH THE SEAFOOD SEASONING AND THE WHITE WINE WHILE YOU PREPARE THE OTHER PARTS OF THE DISH.

3. ADD THE TOMATOES, SOME WINE AND THE ITALIAN SEASONING TO THE PAN AND COOK ON A LOW HEAT

4. IN ANOTHER POT ADD 3 CUPS OF WATER AND BRING TO BOIL. BREAK UP THE PACKAGES OF RAMEN AND ADD TO THE BOILING WATER

5. COOK THE NOODLES UNTIL TENDER BUT STILL FIRM, STIRRING ONCE OR TWICE TO BREAK APART. DRAIN WELL, AND ADD THEM TO BAKING DISH

6. TAKE THE FILLETS AND PLACE THEM IN A BAKING DISH

7. COVER THE FISH AND NOODLES WITH THE SAUCE AND BAKE AT 350 FOR 25 MIN.

NOTES

SEAFOOD CHILI N NOODLES

INGREDIENTS:

- 1 CLOVE - DICED GARLIC
- ½ CUP - DICED ONIONS   } G.O.P.
- ½ CUP - DICED PEPPERS
- 2 PACKAGES - RAMEN NOODLES
- 3 CUPS - WATER
- 1 CUP - COOKED SHRIMP
- 1 CUP - SCALLOPS
- 2-3 - BONELESS AND SKINLESS FISH
- 1 8 OZ CAN - RED BEANS
- 1 8 OZ CAN - BLACK BEANS
- SEASON ALL TO TASTE
- 1 TABLESPOON - EXTRA VIRGIN OLIVE OIL
- 1 CAN - TOMATO SAUCE

DIRECTIONS:

1. IN A LARGE PAN COOK G.O.P. IN SAUCE PAN WITH OLIVE OIL UNTIL BROWNED.

2. ADD SLICES OF FISH, SHRIMP AND SCALLOPS TO THE PAN ALONG WITH SEASON ALL AND COOK THOROUGHLY.

3. IN ANOTHER POT ADD 3 CUPS OF WATER AND BRING TO BOIL. BREAK UP THE PACKAGES OF RAMEN AND ADD TO THE BOILING WATER

4. ONCE THE SEAFOOD IS COOKED ADD THE CANS OF BEANS AND TOMATO AND KEEP IN ON HIGH HEAT FOR 5- 10 MINUTES. THEN LET IT SIMMER FOR 10-20 MIN.

5. COOK THE NOODLES UNTIL TENDER BUT STILL FIRM, STIRRING ONCE OR TWICE TO BREAK APART. DRAIN WELL

6. SET A BED OF NOODLES ON A PLATE THEN TOP WITH THE CHILI.

NOTES

LEMON PEPPER FISH

INGREDIENTS:

- ✻ 1 CLOVE - DICED GARLIC
- ✻ ½ CUP - DICED ONIONS   } G.O.P.
- ✻ ½ CUP - DICED PEPPERS
- ✻ 2 PACKAGES - RAMEN NOODLES
- ✻ 3 CUPS - WATER
- ✻ 4-5 - WHITEFISH AND SOLE FILLETS
- ✻ 1 TABLESPOON - LEMON JUICE
- ✻ 1 TABLESPOON - EXTRA VIRGIN OLIVE OIL
- ✻ LEMON PEPPER SEASONING TO TASTE
- ✻ 2 TABLESPOON - LEMON PEPPER MARINADE
- ✻ 2 CUPS - MIXED VEGETABLES

DIRECTIONS:

1. START BY SEASONING THE FISH WITH THE LEMON PEPPER SEASONING AND LEMON JUICE

2. SAUTÉ THE G.O.P IN A PAN WITH THE OLIVE OIL UNTIL BROWNED THEN ADD THE LEMON PEPPER MARINADE, AND MIXED VEGETABLES, AND MIX WELL UNTIL THE VEGETABLES ARE COOKED THEN PLACE ON SIMMER.

3. IN ANOTHER POT ADD 3 CUPS OF WATER AND BRING TO BOIL. BREAK UP THE PACKAGES OF RAMEN AND ADD TO THE BOILING WATER

4. COOK THE NOODLES UNITL TENDER BUT STILL FIRM, STIRRING ONCE OR TWICE TO BREAK APART. DRAIN WELL, SET THEM INTO THE PAN WITH THE LEMON PEPPER SAUCE AND VEGETABLES.

4. THEN BROWN THE FISH IN ANOTHER PAN UNTILBOTH SIDES, THEN SERVE ON TOP OF A BED OF NOODLES THE NOODLES AND VEGGIES.

NOTES

PAELLA NOODLES

INGREDIENTS:

- 1 CLOVE - DICED GARLIC
- ½ CUP - DICED ONIONS   } G.O.P.
- ½ CUP - DICED PEPPERS
- 2 PACKAGES - RAMEN NOODLES
- 3 CUPS - WATER
- ¼ CUP - SHRIMP
- ¼ CUP - LOBSTER
- ¼ CUP - SQUID
- 1 FRESH - TOMATO DICED
- 1 4 OZ.CAN - TOMATO SAUCE
- ½ CUP - OLIVES
- 1 8 OZ CAN - PEAS
- 1 CUP - CHICKEN BROTH
- 1 TEASPOON - GROUND CUMIN
- ½ A CAN - BEER OR 1/2 CUP - COOKING WINE
- SEASON ALL TO TASTE
- 1 TABLESPOON EXTRA VIRGIN OLIVE OIL

DIRECTIONS:

1. IN A LARGE PAN COOK G.O.P. WITH OLIVE OIL UNTIL BROWNED.

2. ADD THE TOMATOES AND THE TOMATO SAUCE, AND THE WINE OR BEER

3. ADD SEAFOOD MIXTURE TO THE PAN ALONG WITH THE CUMIN AND SEASON ALL*. COOK ON MEDIUM HEAT UNTIL FISH IS COOKED THROUGH.

4. IN ANOTHER POT ADD 3 CUPS OF WATER AND BRING TO BOIL. BREAK UP THE PACKAGES OF RAMEN AND ADD TO THE BOILING WATER

5. ONCE THE SEAFOOD IS ALMOST COOKED LET IT SIMMER.

6. COOK THE NOODLES UNTIL TENDER BUT STILL FIRM, STIRRING ONCE OR TWICE TO BREAK APART. DRAIN WELL

7. SET THE NOODLES BACK INTO THE POT AND ADD THE CHICKEN BROTH, OLIVES, AND PEAS.

8. THEN ADD THE SEAFOOD AND SAUCE TO THE NOODLES AND CONTINUE TO STIR ON A LOW HEAT UNTIL IT THICKENS.

NOTES

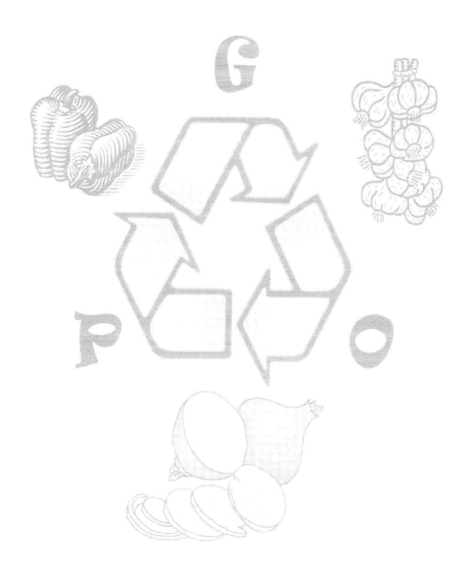

SHRIMP SCAMPI

INGREDIENTS:

- ❊ 1 CLOVE - DICED GARLIC ⎫
- ❊ ½ CUP - DICED ONIONS   ⎬ G.O.P.
- ❊ ½ CUP - DICED PEPPERS ⎭
- ❊ 2 PACKAGES - RAMEN NOODLES
- ❊ 3 CUPS - WATER
- ❊ 1/2 LB. - DEVEINED AND SHELLED SHRIMP
- ❊ 1 TABLESPOON - EXTRA VIRGIN OLIVE OIL
- ❊ SEASON ALL TO TASTE
- ❊ SEAFOOD SEASONING TO TASTE
- ❊ ¼ CUP GRATED ROMANO CHEESE
- ❊ 1 TEASPOON - DRY BASIL
- ❊ 1 TEASPOON - DRY OREGANO

DIRECTIONS:

1. IN A LARGE PAN SAUTÉ G.O.P. WITH OLIVE OIL UNTIL BROWNED.

2. ADD SHRIMP TO THE PAN WITH THE G.O.P ALONG WITH SEASON ALL AND SEAFOOD SEASONING.

3. IN ANOTHER POT ADD 3 CUPS OF WATER AND BRING TO BOIL. BREAK UP THE PACKAGES OF RAMEN AND ADD TO THE BOILING WATER

4. COOK THE NOODLES UNTIL TENDER BUT STILL FIRM, STIRRING ONCE OR TWICE TO BREAK APART. DRAIN WELL, ADD THEM TO THE SHRIMP MIXTURE

5. TOP WITH THE ROMANO CHEESE, BASIL AND OREGANO.

NOTES

CALYPSO NOODLES

INGREDIENTS:

- 1 CAN - MANGO JUICE
- 1 CAN - GUAVA JUICE
- 2 PACKAGES - RAMEN NOODLES
- 3 CUPS - WATER
- 1/2 LB. - DEVEINED AND COOKED SHRIMP (CAN BE BREADED)
- 1 JAR - PEACH APRICOT MARMALADE
- 1 1/2 CUP GRATED COCONUT
- 1 TEASPOON - GUAVA PASTE
- 1 CAN - CRANBERRY SAUCE

DIRECTIONS:

1. IN A SAUCE PAN ADD THE MANGO JUICE AND THE MARMALADE, IN ANOTHER ADD THE CRANBERRY SAUCE, GUAVA JUICE AND PASTE AND COOK IT DOWN OVER A MEDIUM HEAT UNTIL CREAMY.

2. ADD SHRIMP TO THE LARGE BOWL AND POUR THE MANGO/PEACH/APRICOT MIXTURE OVER THEM AND THEN ADD THE COCONUT AND MIX UNTIL THE SHRIMP IS COATED THOROUGHLY

3. SET THE SHRIMP ON A BAKING SHEET AND PUT IN THE OVEN AT 350 DEGREES FOR 15-20 MINS OR UNTIL GOLDEN BROWN.

4. IN ANOTHER POT ADD 3 CUPS OF WATER AND BRING TO BOIL. BREAK UP THE PACKAGES OF RAMEN AND ADD TO THE BOILING WATER

5. COOK THE NOODLES UNTIL TENDER BUT STILL FIRM, STIRRING ONCE OR TWICE TO BREAK APART. DRAIN WELL, ADD THEM TO THE GUAVA/CRANBERRY SAUCE AND MIX WELL UNTIL COATED.

5. SERVE UP THE SHRIMP ON A BED OF THE NOODLES

OODLES OF OPTIONS

CONTRIBUTIONS

NOTES

CHI-CHI'S

BY: T-FISH AND BERTO

INGREDIENTS:

- 1 CLOVE - DICED GARLIC ⎫
- ½ CUP - DICED ONIONS   ⎬ G.O.P.
- ½ CUP - DICED PEPPERS ⎭
- 2 PACKAGES - RAMEN NOODLES
- 3 CUPS - WATER
- 1 BAG - CHEESE DOODLES, OR CORN CHIPS OR NACHO CHEESE DORITOS OR ALL OF THE ABOVE
- 8 OZ. JERKY OR OTHER MEAT STICK, SLICED
- ¼ CUP SHREDDED COLBY, CHEDDAR OR AMERICAN CHEESE
- 1 TABLESPOON OLIVE OIL

DIRECTIONS:
1. SAUTÉ THE G.O.P IN A PAN WITH THE OLIVE OIL AND JERKY SLICES. ONCE BROWNED PLACE ON SIMMER UNTIL NOODLES ARE FINISHED

2. IN ANOTHER POT ADD 3 CUPS OF WATER AND BRING TO BOIL. BREAK UP THE PACKAGES OF RAMEN AND ADD TO THE BOILING WATER

3. COOK THE NOODLES UNTIL TENDER BUT STILL FIRM, STIRRING ONCE OR TWICE TO BREAK APART. DRAIN WELL AND RETURN TO POT.

4. ADD 1/4 CUP OF WATER BACK INTO THE POT, THEN BEGIN TO POUR IN THE CHEESE AND CHEESE DOODLES. BREAK THEM UP AND MIX THEM INTO THE NOODLES UNTIL THEY ARE COATED.

5. ADD THE G.O.P. AND THE JERKY TO THE CHEESY NOODLES; MIX THOROUGHLY.

6. SERVE THIS AS A QUICK AND EASY SNACK

NOTES

BROCCOLI COLESLAW

BY: ANDREA DANKO

INGREDIENTS:

- 2 PACKAGES OF RAMEN NOODLES
- ¾ STICK BUTTER
- ¾ CUP OLIVE OIL
- ¼ CUP SLICED ALMONDS
- ¼ CUP CIDER VINEGAR
- ¼ CUP BROWN SUGAR
- 2 PACKAGES BROCCOLI SLAW
- ¼ CUP SUNFLOWER SEEDS
- ALL PURPOSE SEASONING - TO TASTE
- SCALLIONS SLICES

DIRECTIONS:

1. START BY COOKING THE CRUMBLED NOODLES AND BUTTER TOGETHER UNTIL BROWNED AND THEN ADD THE SLICED ALMONDS

2. IN A SEPARATE BOWL MIX THE OLIVE OIL, CIDER VINEGAR, BROWN SUGAR AND ALL PURPOSE SEASONING TOGETHER TO CREATE A MARINADE.

3. OPEN THE PACKAGES OF THE BROCCOLI SLAW AND POUR THE MARINADE IN IT AND THE MIX IN THE NOODLES

4. ONCE THE MIXTURE IS COATED WITH THE MARINADE ADD THE SUNFLOWER SEEDS, THEN TOP WITH CUT UP SCALLIONS

C12

NOTES

ASIAN CABBAGE SALAD

BY: JANENE BEATTIE & ROBIN LAUFFER

INGREDIENTS:

SALAD:

- 4 PACKAGES – RAMEN NOODLES, CRUSHED
- 1 HEAD – RED CABBAGE, CHOPPED
- 2 BUNCHES – GREEN ONIONS, CHOPPED
- 1/2 CUP – SLICED ALMONDS
- ½ CUP – SESAME SEEDS

DRESSING:

- ½ TEASPOON SALT
- 1 TEASPOON PEPPER
- 2 TEASPOONS ACCENT
- ¼ CUP SUGAR
- ¾ CUP OLIVE OIL
- ½ CUP RICE VINEGAR (WHITE)

DIRECTIONS:

1. IN A LARGE SALAD BOWL ,TOSS THE RAMEN, CABBAGE, GREEN ONIONS, ALMONDS AND SESAME SEEDS

2. MIX THE DRESSING INGREDIENTS IN A SCREW TOP JAR, THEN COVER AND SHAKE WELL. POUR OVER SALAD JUST BEFORE SERVING.

NOTES

CHEESE NOODLES

BY: BRIAN HOGUE & MIKE DILLARD

INGREDIENTS:

* 2 PACKAGES - RAMEN NOODLES
* 3 CUPS - WATER
* ¼ STICK - BUTTER
* 1 TABLESPOON - OLIVE OIL
* 3-4 SLICES - AMERICAN CHEESE (WHITE OR YELLOW)
* 1 CUP - MILK
* SALT - TO TASTE
* PEPPER - TO TASTE
* FEEL FREE TO ADD OTHER CHEESES: MOZZARELLA, MONTERREY JACK, COLBY, PARMESAN, ETC.

DIRECTIONS:

1. IN A POT ADD 3 CUPS OF WATER AND BRING TO BOIL. BREAK UP THE PACKAGES OF RAMEN AND ADD TO THE BOILING WATER

2. COOK THE NOODLES UNTIL TENDER BUT STILL FIRM, STIRRING ONCE OR TWICE TO BREAK APART. DRAIN WELL. ADD THE MILK AND THE BUTTER AND CONTINUE TO STIR UNTIL THE BUTTER IS MELTED.

3. THEN ADD IN THE CHEESES AND THE SALT AND PEPPER AND MIX UNTIL CREAMY.

NOTES

ADOBO CHICKEN N' NOODLES

CREATED FOR MY FACEBOOK GROUP: I LOVE RAMEN AND ONE OF MY FAVORITE FILIPINO DISHES

INGREDIENTS:

- EXTRA VIRGIN OLIVE OIL
- 1 ENTIRE HEAD - DICED GARLIC
- ½ CUP - DICED ONIONS
- ½ CUP - DICED MULTI-COLORED PEPPERS } G.O.P.
- 2 PACKAGES OF RAMEN NOODLES
- 1 3LB. CHICKEN - CUT INTO PIECES
- SEASON ALL - TO TASTE
- 3 CUPS - WATER
- ½ CUP - SOY SAUCE
- ½ CUP - WHITE COOKING WINE
- 3-4 - WHOLE ALL SPICE

DIRECTIONS:

1. SPRINKLE SEASON ALL ON ALL THE CHICKEN PIECES. PLACE CHICKEN IN A SLOW COOKER. IN A SMALL BOWL MIX THE HALF OF THE GARLIC, ONIONS, AND PEPPERS IN WITH THE SOY SAUCE, WINE, ALL SPICE AND VINEGAR, AND POUR OVER THE CHICKEN. COOK ON LOW FOR 6 TO 8 HOURS.

2. IN A LARGE FRYING PAN COOK THE OTHER HALF OF THE GARLIC, ONIONS, AND PEPPERS WITH THE OLIVE OIL. ONCE BROWNED REDUCE HEAT TO SIMMER UNTIL NOODLES ARE FINISHED.

3. IN ANOTHER PAN ADD 3 CUPS OF WATER AND BRING TO BOIL. BREAK UP THE PACKAGES OF RAMEN AND ADD TO BOILING WATER.

4. COOK THE NOODLES UNTIL TENDER BUT STILL FIRM, STIRRING ONCE OR TWICE TO BREAK APART. DRAIN WELL.

5. ADD THE NOODLES TO THE PAN WITH THE SAUTÉED INGREDIENTS AND MIX THEM ALL TOGETHER WITH SOME OLIVE OIL.

6. ONCE THE CHICKEN IS FINISHED, SET THE NOODLES ON A PLATE ADD THE CHICKEN ON TOP AND POUR THE SAUCE OVER THE CHICKEN AND THE NOODLES AND ENJOY!!

NOTES

RAMEN BAKLAVA

INSPIRED BY: ONE OF MY FAVORITE DISHES THAT COMES IN ALL FORMS THROUGHOUT THE MIDDLE EAST AND THE MEDITERRANEAN.

INGREDIENTS:

- 2 CUPS - CHOPPED NUTS
- ½ CUP - BUTTER
- 2 TSP - CINNAMON
- 1 TSP - VANILLA EXTRACT
- 2 PACKAGES - RAMEN NOODLES
- ½ CUP - BROWN SUGAR
- ½ CUP - HONEY
- 4 CUPS - WATER
- ½ CUP - WILD TURKEY -AMERICAN HONEY (WHISKEY/BOURBON BLEND)

DIRECTIONS:

1. BUTTER THE BOTTOM A BAKING PAN. PRE HEAT THE OVEN TO 350 °F.

2. CHOP UP THE NUTS AND TOSS WITH 1 TSP. CINNAMON AND SET ASIDE.

3. BRING THE WATER TO A BOIL IN A POT AND COOK THE NOODLES WHOLE UNTIL THE BUNDLE OF NOODLES CAN BE UNFOLDED. REMOVE THEM FROM THE WATER ONCE THEY ARE READY. DRAIN WELL.

4. SET THE FIRST BUNDLE INTO THE PAN AND UNFOLD AND BUTTER THOROUGHLY. TAKE ONE CUP OF CHOPPED NUTS AND COVER THE 1ST LAYER. SET THE NEXT BUNDLE ON TOP AND REPEAT THE SAME SEQUENCE.

5. BEFORE THE BAKLAVA GOES INTO THE OVEN, SOAK THE NOODLES WITH THE AMERICAN HONEY LIQUOR. BAKE IN THE OVEN FOR APPROXIMATELY 50 MIN, UNTIL GOLDEN BROWN AND CRISPY ON TOP.

6. WHILE THE BAKLAVA IS BAKING YOU CAN MAKE THE SAUCE. BOIL THE WATER THEN ADD THE SUGAR AND MIX UNTIL MELTED. ADD THE VANILLA AND HONEY AND SIMMER FOR 20 MINS.

7. REMOVE THE PAN FROM THE OVEN AND DRIZZLE THE SAUCE OVER TOP OF IT AND LET IT COOL. SERVE AT ROOM TEMPERATURE. ENJOY!!

NOTES

RAMEN IN A SPINACH ARTICHOKE SAUCE

INSPIRED BY: EVERY RESTAURANT CHAIN'S POPULAR APPETIZER

INGREDIENTS:

- 1 TBS. - EXTRA VIRGIN OLIVE OIL
- 1 CLOVE - MINCED GARLIC
- ½ CUP - FINELY CHOPPED ONIONS
- 1½ CUPS - ALFREDO SAUCE
- 2 PACKAGES OF RAMEN NOODLES
- 1 8OZ JAR - SOUR CREAM
- SEASON ALL - TO TASTE
- 3 CUPS - WATER
- 1 10OZ. PACKAGE - FROZEN CHOPPED SPINACH
- 1 CUP - PARMESAN OR ROMANO CHEESE
- ¼ TEASPOON - PAPRIKA
- 1 CUP - DICED TOMATOES
- ¼ CUP - FRESH DICED PARSLEY OR BASIL

DIRECTIONS:

1. WARM OIL IN A PAN ON A MEDIUM HEAT. THEN ADD THE ONIONS AND GARLIC AND COOK THEM UNTIL THEY ARE SOFT.

2. REDUCE THE HEAT TO MEDIUM-LOW AND ADD THE REMAINING INGREDIENTS EXCEPT THE RAMEN AND WATER. COOK UNTIL HEATED THROUGH.

3. IN ANOTHER PAN ADD 3 CUPS OF WATER AND BRING TO BOIL. BREAK UP THE PACKAGES OF RAMEN AND ADD TO BOILING WATER.

4. COOK THE NOODLES UNTIL TENDER BUT STILL FIRM, STIRRING ONCE OR TWICE TO BREAK APART. DRAIN WELL

5. ADD THE NOODLES TO THE PAN WITH THE SAUTÉED INGREDIENTS AND MIX THEM ALL TOGETHER WELL. SERVE UP ON A PLATE AND SPRINKLE TOMATOES AND PARSLEY OR BASIL ON TOP.

NOTES

GARLIC RAMEN BRUSCHETTA

INGREDIENTS:

- EXTRA VIRGIN OLIVE OIL
- 1 CLOVE - DICED GARLIC
- ½ CUP - DICED ONIONS
- ½ CUP - DICED MULTI-COLORED PEPPERS
- 2 PACKAGES - RAMEN NOODLES
- 5 DICED - ROMA TOMATOES
- 2 TBSP - ITALIAN SEASONING
- 3 CUPS - WATER
- 4-5 LEAVES - FRESH BASIL DICED
- FRESH MOZZARELLA CHEESE
- 2 TSP - PESTO

DIRECTIONS:

1. IN A LARGE FRYING PAN COOK THE GARLIC, ONIONS, AND PEPPERS WITH THE OLIVE OIL. ONCE BROWNED REDUCE HEAT TO SIMMER UNTIL NOODLES ARE FINISHED.

2. IN ANOTHER PAN ADD 3 CUPS OF WATER AND BRING TO BOIL. BREAK UP THE PACKAGES OF RAMEN AND ADD TO BOILING WATER.

3. COOK THE NOODLES UNTIL TENDER BUT STILL FIRM, STIRRING ONCE OR TWICE TO BREAK APART. DRAIN WELL.

4. ADD THE NOODLES TO THE PAN WITH THE SAUTÉED VEGETABLES ALONG WITH THE PESTO,CHEESE, AND ITALIAN SEASONING.

5. ADD ALL THE INGREDIENTS INTO A SERVING BOWL WITH THE TOMATOES AND BASIL AND MIX WELL AND THEN TOP WITH THE FRESH BASIL. SERVE UP IT AND ENJOY!!

C18

NOTES

FIESTA NOODLES

INGREDIENTS:

- EXTRA VIRGIN OLIVE OIL
- 1 CLOVE - DICED GARLIC
- ½ CUP - DICED ONIONS
- 2 CUPS - DICED MULTI-COLORED PEPPERS
- 2 PACKAGES - RAMEN NOODLES
- ½ CAN - BLACK BEANS, DRAINED AND HEATED
- 12 OZ - UNCOOKED SHRIMP
- 3 CUPS - WATER
- ½ TSP - CUMIN
- ½ - AVOCADO, SLICED THIN
- CAYENNE PEPPER AND SAZON SEASONING - TO TASTE

DIRECTIONS:

1. IN A LARGE FRYING PAN COOK THE GARLIC, ONIONS, AND PEPPERS WITH THE OLIVE OIL. ONCE BROWNED REDUCE HEAT TO SIMMER UNTIL NOODLES ARE FINISHED.

2. IN ANOTHER PAN ADD 3 CUPS OF WATER AND BRING TO BOIL. BREAK UP THE PACKAGES OF RAMEN AND ADD TO BOILING WATER.

3. COOK THE NOODLES UNTIL TENDER BUT STILL FIRM, STIRRING ONCE OR TWICE TO BREAK APART. DRAIN WELL.

4. ADD THE NOODLES TO THE PAN WITH THE SAUTÉED VEGETABLES ALONG WITH THE SHRIMP AND BLACK BEANS, CAYENNE PEPPER AND THE SAZON AND MIX WELL UNTIL THE SHRIMP ARE COOKED.

5. THEN SERVE IT UP AND GARNISH WITH THE AVOCADO. . .ENJOY!!

NOTES

RED VELVET RAMEN

INSPIRED BY: THE FAMOUS CAKE MAN RAVEN RED VELVET CAKE.

INGREDIENTS:

- 2 TBSP - UNSWEETENED COCOA POWDER
- 2 OZ - RED FOOD COLORING
- 1 CUP - BUTTERMILK
- 1 TSP - VANILLA EXTRACT
- 2 PACKAGES - RAMEN NOODLES
- 1-1/2 CUPS - WHITE SUGAR
- ½ CUP - MIXED NUTS-GRATED
- 3 CUPS - WATER
- CREAM CHEESE FROSTING - TO TASTE

DIRECTIONS:

1. GREASE A 9" SQUARE PAN. PRE HEAT THE OVEN TO 350 ° F. IN A LARGE BOWL MAKE A PASTE OF THE COCOA AND RED FOOD COLORING

2. COMBINE THE BUTTERMILK AND VANILLA EXTRACT TO THE PASTE. THEN MIX IN THE SUGAR AND STIR UNTIL BLENDED WELL.

3. BRING THE WATER TO A BOIL IN A POT AND COOK THE NOODLES WHOLE UNTIL THE BUNDLE OF NOODLES CAN BE UNFOLDED. REMOVE THEM FROM THE WATER ONCE THEY ARE READY. DRAIN WELL.

4. SOAK THE NOODLES IN THE COCOA SAUCE UNTIL COATED THOROUGHLY

5. SET EACH BUNDLE INTO THE PAN AND UNFOLD. DECIDE WHICH ONE YOU WANT TO BE THE BOTTOM HALF AND SPRINKLE THE MIXED NUTS OVER TOP. BAKE IN THE OVEN FOR 10-12 MINS. REMOVE ONCE THE SAUCE HAS DRIED UP AND THE NOODLES ARE SOLID ENOUGH TO BE REMOVED FROM THE PAN IN ONE PIECE.

6. ONCE THE NOODLES ARE COOLED COAT THE BOTTOM LAYER WITH ICING AND THEN STACK THE OTHER BUNDLE ON TOP AND ICE THAT LAYER. THIS CAN BE CUT INTO VARIOUS SIZES AND SERVED WITH A GARNISH OF YOUR CHOICE.

NOTES

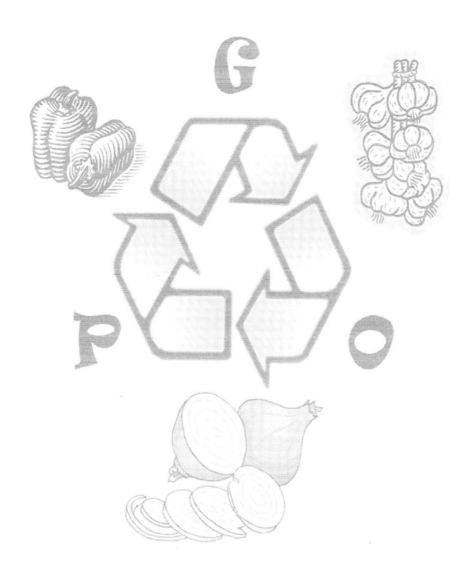

NOTES

NOTES

NOTES

SPECIAL THANKS

FIRST AND FOREMOST I WANT TO THANK TO GOD FOR GIVING ME THE PEACE OF MIND TO TAKE ON THIS CHALLENGING PROJECT AND PURSUE A GOAL THAT I NEVER DREAMED OF.

THANKS ARE DUE TO MY FAMILY AND FRIENDS FOR PROVIDING THE REASSURANCE THAT I NEEDED TO TAKE THIS ON. THEY REALLY PUSHED ME AND KEPT MY SPIRITS LIFTED DURING THE TRYING TIMES OF THIS PROJECT. THEIR LOVE AND SUPPORT KEPT ME GOING AND REALLY INSPIRED ME TO PURSUE ANY AND ALL OF MY DREAMS.

THANK YOU ALL AS WELL TO MY TEAM FOR BELIEVING ME AND GRABBING A HOLD OF MY VISION AND PUSHING ME THROUGH TO COMPLETE THIS BOOK. YOU PUSHED ME TO REACH NEW LEVELS AND REALLY TAP INTO ALL THE POTENTIAL THAT THIS PROJECT HAD.

SPECIAL THANKS TO MY GRAPHICS CONSULTANT MISTIE ROBERTS. YOU WERE A GREAT CRITIC OF MY GRAPHIC WORK AND REALLY HELPED CREATE THE IMAGES THAT WERE STUCK IN MY HEAD THAT I WANTED TO SHARE WITH MY EVERYONE. SHE CAN BE FOUND AT: WWW.SCOOPDESIGNS.COM

ALSO THANKS GO OUT TO MARY GOETZ FOR THE GREAT EDITING JOB. YOU REALLY GAVE ME A GREAT PERSPECTIVE ON WHAT I WAS SAYING AND HOW TO PRESENT MY IDEAS CLEARLY. YOUR FEEDBACK REALLY HELPED ME REFINE AND FINALIZE MY RECIPES.

BIG THANKS ARE ALSO DUE FOR THE KIND WORDS AND ADVICE FROM RON KONZAK THE AUTHOR OF _THE BOOK OF RAMEN_. THE BIGGEST PART OF ME GOING THROUGH WITH WRITING THIS HAD TO DO WITH THE IRONY OF ME RESEARCHING THIS TYPE OF BOOK AND FINDING A MAN THAT SHARES THE SAME FIRST NAME AS ME (RON), SHARES THE SAME PROFESSION AS ME (ARCHITECTURE), HAS A SHARED INTEREST IN THE SAME TYPE OF ARCHITECTURE (JAPANESE), AND MOST OF ALL WROTE A BOOK ABOUT RAMEN. HIS WISE WORDS AND ADVICE GIVEN FROM THE OTHER SIDE OF THE COUNTRY, WITH US NEVER MEETING INSPIRED ME TO GO FORWARD AND COMPLETE WHAT I HAVE SHARED WITH YOU.

ALSO THANKS GO TO MY FRIEND/PROFESSOR J.MICHAEL KELLY FOR HELPING ME FIND A WAY TO GET THIS BOOK PUBLISHED AND IN PRINT. YOU ALWAYS PUSHED ME TO THINK OUTSIDE OF THE BOX IN THE WORLD OF ARCHITECTURE AND LIFE. WITHOUT YOU AND YOUR BROTHER SCOTT, THIS WOULD NOT HAVE REACHED THE MASSES.

About The Author

RONALD A. MOSS II IS AN ARCHITECTURAL DESIGNER/CONSULTANT WHO HAS ENJOYED FOLLOWING HIS DREAMS OF ENTREPRENEURSHIP. HIS PATH THAT BEGAN IN THE ARCHITECTURAL FIELD AND LEAD INTO COST AND PROJECT MANAGEMENT, STARTED IN WESTERN PA, A PLACE THAT PREPARED HIM FOR THE PEAKS AND VALLEYS AHEAD. IT WAS THERE THAT HIS CREATIVITY, HUMANITARIANISM AND DESIRES TO TURN PEOPLE'S IDEAS AND DREAMS INTO CONCRETE REALITY WERE BIRTHED. THERE HIS PASSION FOR THE ARTS INCLUDING: CULINARY ARTS, AND LITERATURE AS WELL AS ARCHITECTURE/DESIGN AND CONSTRUCTION WAS SPARKED.

RONALD GREW UP IN NEW KENSINGTON, PA HE SPENT HIS EARLY YEARS PARTICIPATING IN A VARIETY OF ACADEMIC AND EXTRA-CIRCULAR ACTIVITIES THAT HELPED HIM TO CULTIVATE HIS PROBLEM SOLVING FACULTIES, SOCIAL SKILLS AND PHILANTHROPIC SENSIBILITIES. THESE HELPED SHAPE HIS PASSION, DETERMINATION AND DRIVE TO LET NOTHING STAND BETWEEN HIM AND THE FULFILLMENT OF HIS DREAMS AND HIS PURSUIT OF HELPING OTHERS ACHIEVE THEIRS.

RONALD IS NOW ENTERING A NEW AND EXCITING PHASE OF HIS PROFESSIONAL LIFE, ONE WHERE HE SEEKS TO DEVELOP INNOVATIVE PROJECTS THAT EXTEND TO AREAS OUTSIDE THE REALM OF ARCHITECTURE. HIS FIRST INITIATIVE TO BECOME AN AUTHOR, FOLLOWED HIS GRADUATION FROM TEMPLE UNIVERSITY WITH A BACHELORS OF ARCHITECTURE DEGREE. HE THEN NEEDED DIVERSITY IN HIS CREATIVE ACTIVITIES AND AFTER THE SUCCESS OF A FRIEND OF HIS, MICHAEL ABDUL-QAWI, WHO HAD SELF-PUBLISHED A COLLECTION OF SHORT STORIES ENTITLED <u>SICK WITH LOVE</u>, HE DECIDED TO TAKE UP THE PERSONAL CHALLENGE AND WRITE A COOKBOOK.

UPON COMPLETING HIS FIRST COOKBOOK ENTITLED: <u>OODLES OF OPTIONS: THE SURVIVAL GUIDE TO LIFE OUTSIDE OF YOUR MOTHER'S KITCHEN</u>, RONALD IS VERY EXCITED FOR THE FUTURE. HE HOPES IT PROVIDES HIM WITH THE OPPORTUNITY TO SHARE MANY OF THE LESSONS HE HAS LEARNED,FROM HIS FAMILY, IN THE KITCHEN WITH PEOPLE OF ALL AGES AND FROM ALL OVER TO HELP THEM APPLY THESE LESSONS TO ALL TYPES OF DISHES. HIS LOVE FOR DELICIOUS AND EXCITING CUISINE AND HIS DRIVE TO PUSH THE LIMITS HAS PRODUCED THIS COLLECTION OF RECIPES THAT APPEAL TO PEOPLE OF ALL AGES AND CAN BE ADAPTED TO SUIT YOUR OWN PERSONAL TASTES.

Made in the USA
Charleston, SC
11 April 2013